WJEC French

Teacher Guide

Louise Pearce, Bethan McHugh
and Chris Whittaker

Crown House Publishing
www.crownhouse.co.uk

Endorsed by
wjec cbac

First published by
Crown House Publishing Ltd
Crown Buildings, Bancyfelin, Carmarthen, Wales, SA33 5ND, UK
www.crownhouse.co.uk
and
Crown House Publishing Company LLC
PO Box 2223
Williston, VT 05495
www.crownhousepublishing.com

British Library of Cataloguing-in-Publication Data

A catalogue entry for this book is available from the British Library.

An extension of this page appears on page 119.

ISBN 978-178583092-1

CONTENTS

WJEC GCSE FRENCH

THEMES

WJEC GCSE French is divided into three main **themes**. Each theme has three sub-themes which are divided into modules. This makes a total of 18 modules to be studied during the course. The book is divided up in the same way and each sub-theme contains:

- Three double pages of activities for each module.
- Double pages of vocabulary for each module.
- 'Grammar in context' exercises at the end of the sub-theme.

IDENTITY AND CULTURE	WALES AND THE WORLD – AREAS OF INTEREST	CURRENT AND FUTURE STUDY AND EMPLOYMENT
YOUTH CULTURE • Self and relationships • Technology and social media	**HOME AND LOCALITY** • Local areas of interest • Travel and transport	**CURRENT STUDY** • School/college life • School/college studies
LIFESTYLE • Health and fitness • Entertainment and leisure	**THE WIDER WORLD** • Local and regional features and characteristics of France and French-speaking countries • Holidays and tourism	**ENTERPRISE, EMPLOYABILITY AND FUTURE PLANS** • Employment • Skills and personal qualities • Post-16 study • Career plans
CUSTOMS AND TRADITIONS • Food and drink • Festivals and celebrations	**GLOBAL SUSTAINABILITY** • Environment • Social issues	

SUMMARY OF ASSESSMENT

Remember that the exam is divided up equally across the four skill areas: reading, listening, speaking and writing. Each exam is worth 25% and all the exams will cover all three themes. Dictionaries are not allowed in any part of the exam.

UNIT 1: SPEAKING

- 12 minutes' preparation time
- 7–9 minutes (Foundation tier)
- 10–12 minutes (Higher tier)
- 60 marks
- Role play (15 marks) on one of the three themes
- Photo card discussion (15 marks) on a different theme with two seen and two unseen questions
- Conversation (30 marks) on two themes (one of which the student chooses in advance and one of which must cover the third theme not covered in the role play and photo card discussion)

UNIT 2: LISTENING

- 35 minutes (Foundation tier) including 5 minutes' reading time
- 45 minutes (Higher tier) including 5 minutes' reading time
- 45 marks
- A range of questions in English
- Two questions in the assessed language
- Three overlap questions between Foundation and Higher
- Question types include: multiple choice with non-verbal and written responses, gap-fill one word answers, selecting correct/false statements and short answer responses
- Different types of spoken language including monologues, conversations, discussions, interviews, announcements and messages

UNIT 3: READING

- 1 hour (Foundation tier)
- 1 hour 15 minutes (Higher tier)
- 60 marks
- A range of questions in English
- Three questions in the assessed language
- Two questions based on literary texts
- Two overlap questions between Foundation and Higher
- Question types include: multiple choice with non-verbal responses, match-up responses, gap-fill one word answers, selecting correct/false statements, short answer responses, completing information in a table and longer responses
- A range of contexts including adverts, newspaper articles (adapted), literary-type texts (adapted), e-mails, messages and letters
- A translation into English (35–40 words for Foundation and 50–55 words for Higher)

UNIT 4: WRITING

- 1 hour 15 minutes (Foundation tier)
- 1 hour 30 minutes (Higher tier)
- 60 marks
- A short response in the assessed language (Foundation)
- A short text of approximately 50 words (Foundation)
- An extended piece of writing of approximately 100 words such as an e-mail, letter or promotional material (Foundation and Higher)
- An extended more complex piece of writing of approximately 150 words such as a letter, e-mail, web page, article or report (Higher)
- A translation from English into French (35–40 words at Foundation, 50–55 at Higher)

SCOPE OF STUDY

According to the Department for Education Modern Foreign Languages GCSE Subject Content (December 2015)* and the WJEC GCSE specification, students should be able to do the following:

SPEAKING: COMMUNICATE AND INTERACT EFFECTIVELY IN SPEECH

- Communicate and interact effectively in speech for a variety of purposes across a range of specified contexts.
- Take part in a short conversation, asking and answering questions, and exchanging opinions.
- Convey information and narrate events coherently and confidently, using and adapting language for new purposes.
- Speak spontaneously, responding to unexpected questions, points of view or situations, sustaining communication by using rephrasing or repair strategies, as appropriate.
- Initiate and develop conversations and discussion, producing extended sequences of speech.
- Make appropriate and accurate use of a variety of vocabulary and grammatical structures, including some more complex forms, with reference to past, present and future events.
- Make creative and more complex use of the language, as appropriate, to express and justify their own thoughts and points of view.

LISTENING: UNDERSTAND AND RESPOND TO DIFFERENT TYPES OF SPOKEN LANGUAGE

- Identify the overall message, key points, details and opinions in a variety of short and longer spoken passages, involving some more complex language, recognising the relationship between past, present and future events.
- Deduce meaning from a variety of short and longer spoken texts, involving some complex language and more abstract material, including short narratives and authentic material addressing a wide range of relevant contemporary and cultural themes.
- Recognise and respond to key information, important themes and ideas in more extended spoken text, including authentic sources, adapted and abridged, as appropriate, by being able to answer questions, extract information, evaluate and draw conclusions.

---

* See: https://www.gov.uk/government/uploads/system/uploads/attachments_data/file/485567/GCSE_subject_content_modern_foreign_langs.pdf

READING: UNDERSTAND AND RESPOND TO DIFFERENT TYPES OF WRITTEN LANGUAGE

- Identify the overall message, key points, details and opinions in a variety of short and longer written passages, involving some more complex language, recognising the relationship between past, present and future events.
- Deduce meaning from a variety of short and longer written texts from a range of specified contexts, including authentic sources involving some complex language and unfamiliar material, as well as short narratives and authentic material addressing a wide range of relevant contemporary and cultural themes.
- Recognise and respond to key information, important themes and ideas in more extended written text and authentic sources, including some extracts from relevant abridged or adapted literary texts.
- Demonstrate understanding by being able to scan for particular information, organise and present relevant details, draw inferences in context and recognise implicit meaning where appropriate.
- Translate a short passage from the assessed language into English.

WRITING: COMMUNICATE IN WRITING

- Write short texts, using simple sentences and familiar language accurately to convey meaning and exchange information.
- Produce clear and coherent text of extended length to present facts and express ideas and opinions appropriately for different purposes and in different settings.
- Describe and narrate with reference to past, present and future events.
- Make independent, creative and more complex use of the language, as appropriate, to note down key points, express and justify individual thoughts and points of view, in order to interest, inform or convince.
- Translate sentences and short texts from English into the assessed language to convey key messages accurately and to apply grammatical knowledge of language and structures in context.

CONTEXT AND PURPOSES

The WJEC GCSE French textbook gives comprehensive coverage of the context and purposes identified by the Department for Education. Students are expected to:

- Understand and use language across a range of contexts, appropriate to their age, interests and maturity levels.
- Use language for a variety of purposes and with a variety of different audiences, including for personal, academic and employment related use.
- Make use of appropriate social conventions, including informal and formal address and register, as relevant to the task.
- Students will be expected to understand different types of spoken language, including recorded input from one or more speakers in public and social settings and recorded material from authentic sources and the media, appropriate to this level.
- Students will be expected to understand different types of written language, including relevant personal communication, public information, factual and literary texts, appropriate to this level.
- Study literary texts, including extracts and excerpts, adapted and abridged as appropriate, from poems, letters, short stories, essays, novels or plays from contemporary and historical sources.

GRAMMAR REQUIREMENTS

This is the list of grammar requirements for Foundation and Higher students, as specified by the Department for Education. Remember that for structures marked (R) only receptive knowledge is required, but these are the grammar points that examiners are usually referring to when they are talking about 'complex language'. The textbook covers all of these points within the context of the themes and sub-themes and also has a comprehensive grammar glossary with verb tables at the end of the book.

FRENCH (FOUNDATION TIER)

Nouns:

- gender
- singular and plural forms

Articles:

- definite, indefinite and partitive, including use of *de* after negatives

Adjectives:

- agreement
- position
- comparative and superlative: regular and *meilleur*
- demonstrative (*ce, cet, cette, ces*)
- indefinite (*chaque, quelque*)
- possessive

Adverbs:

- comparative and superlative
- regular
- interrogative (*comment, quand*)
- adverbs of time and place (*aujourd'hui, demain, ici, là-bas*)
- common adverbial phrases

Quantifiers/intensifiers:

- *très, assez, beaucoup, peu, trop*

Pronouns:

- personal: all subjects, including *on*
- reflexive
- relative: *qui*
- relative: *que* (R)
- object: direct (R) and indirect (R)
- position and order of object pronouns (R)
- disjunctive/emphatic
- demonstrative (*ça, cela*)
- indefinite (*quelqu'un*)
- interrogative (*qui, que*)
- use of *y, en* (R)

Verbs:

- regular and irregular verbs, including reflexive verbs
- all persons of the verb, singular and plural
- negative forms
- interrogative forms
- modes of address: *tu*, *vous*
- impersonal verbs (*il faut*)
- verbs followed by an infinitive, with or without a preposition
- tenses
- present
- perfect
- imperfect: *avoir*, *être* and *faire*
- other common verbs in the imperfect tense (R)
- immediate future
- future (R)
- conditional: *vouloir* and *aimer*
- pluperfect (R)
- passive voice: present tense (R)
- imperative
- present participle (R)

Prepositions:

- common prepositions e.g. *à, au, à l', à la, aux; de, du, de l', de la, des; après; avant; avec; chez; contre; dans; depuis; derrière; devant; entre; pendant; pour; sans; sur; sous; vers*
- common compound prepositions e.g. *à côté de; près de; en face de; à cause de; au lieu de*

Conjunctions:

- common coordinating conjunctions e.g. *car*; *donc*; *ensuite; et; mais; ou; ou bien; puis*
- common subordinating conjunctions e.g. *comme; lorsque; parce que; puisque; quand; que; si*

Number, quantity, dates and time:

- including use of *depuis* with present tense

FRENCH (HIGHER TIER)

All grammar and structures listed for Foundation tier, as well as:

Adjectives:

- comparative and superlative, including *meilleur*, *pire*

Adverbs:

- comparative and superlative, including *mieux*, *le mieux*

Pronouns:

- use of *y*, *en*
- relative: *que*
- relative: *dont* (R)
- object: direct and indirect
- position and order of object pronouns
- demonstrative (*celui*) (R)
- possessive (*le mien*) (R)

Verbs:

- tenses
- future
- imperfect
- conditional
- pluperfect
- passive voice: future, imperfect and perfect tenses (R)
- perfect infinitive
- present participle, including use after *en*
- subjunctive mood: present, in commonly used expressions (R)

Time:

- including use of *depuis* with imperfect tense

INTRODUCING THE WJEC GCSE FRENCH TEXTBOOK

This textbook has been designed in conjunction with WJEC to offer engaging and relevant content with comprehensive coverage of the WJEC themes and sub-themes, incorporating all of the new exam components.

The modules have been designed for mixed-ability teaching and include a wide range of activities of varying ability to practise all four skills at both Foundation and Higher level.

Throughout the student book you will see the following icons:

READING

Each module (e.g. 1a Self and relationships) has six reading exercises which include:

- Three shorter reading tasks
- Three longer reading tasks
- Two tasks in the assessed language
- One task on a literary text based on the module
- Verbal and non-verbal questions
- Questions addressing the requirements of the Department for Education scope of study and context and purposes requirements

In addition, there is a translation into English in every module.

LISTENING

Each module contains three listening tasks, one of which is in the assessed language. They cover a range of contexts and use a variety of question styles in order to match the regulatory requirements for the exam.

SPEAKING

Every module contains:

- A photo card with practice questions. The real exam has two seen and two unseen questions. For practice, the photo cards in the textbook have five questions which increase in difficulty to help Foundation and Higher candidates to prepare for the exam.

- The role play in the exam has five interactions including one unpredictable question. In order to help students prepare for this element of the exam, the role play tasks in the textbook have six prompts (two statements, two questions to ask and two tense statements) for students to practise, which will help them get used to the pressures of the preparation time before their speaking exam.
- A list of suggested conversation questions. Each module has six questions which increase in difficulty and will require detailed opinions and a range of tenses. These can form part of a bank of questions to help students revise for this element of the exam.

WRITING

Every module contains carefully structured tasks that are similar in demand to the writing exam. These vary in style to correspond to the requirements of the real exam and can all be adapted to suit Foundation and Higher students. There is also a translation into French in every module.

EXTRA

Some exercises have an Extra section which offers extra language practice or some more challenging questions. These are ideal to stretch and challenge more able pupils.

GRAMMAR

Grammar boxes throughout the modules highlight relevant points that are raised. There is also a 'Grammar in context' section at the end of every sub-theme (two modules) with practice exercises as well as a grammar glossary with verb tables at the back of the book.

Key words, phrases or reminders are identified by this icon throughout the book.

At the end of every module there is a list of useful vocabulary which is based on the WJEC GCSE specification.

TEXTBOOK OVERVIEW

	Identity and culture	Wales and the world – areas of interest	Current and future study and employment
Unit 1 Modules 1–3	**Youth culture** (1a) Self and relationships (1b) Technology and social media	**Home and locality** (2a) Local areas of interest (2b) Travel and transport	**Current study** (3a) School/college life (3b) School/college studies
Unit 2 Modules 4–6	**Lifestyle** (4a) Health and fitness (4b) Entertainment and leisure	**The wider world** (5a) Local and regional features and characteristics of France and French-speaking countries (5b) Holidays and tourism	**Enterprise, employability and future plans** (6a) Employment (6b) Skills and personal qualities
Unit 3 Modules 7–9	**Customs and traditions** (7a) Food and drink (7b) Festivals and celebrations	**Global sustainability** (8a) Environment (8b) Social issues	**Enterprise, employability and future plans** (9a) Post-16 study (9b) Career plans

TWO YEAR PROGRAMME OF STUDY

	Term 1	Term 2	Term 3
Year 10	Introduction to GCSE MFL Grammar revision	Home and locality (Modules 2a and 2b)	Lifestyle (Modules 4a and 4b)
	Youth culture (Modules 1a and 1b)	Current study (Modules 3a and 3b)	The wider world (Modules 5a and 5b)
Year 11	Enterprise, employability and future plans (Modules 6a and 6b)	Global sustainability (Modules 8a and 8b)	Oral exam Revision
	Customs and traditions (Modules 7a and 7b)	Enterprise, employability and future plans (Modules 9a and 9b)	

THREE YEAR PROGRAMME OF STUDY

	Term 1	Term 2	Term 3
Year 9	Introduction to GCSE MFL	Home and locality (Modules 2a and 2b)	Lifestyle (Modules 4a and 4b)
	Youth culture (Modules 1a and 1b)	Current study (Modules 3a and 3b)	The wider world (Modules 5a and 5b)
Year 10	Enterprise, employability and future plans (Modules 6a and 6b)	Global sustainability (Modules 8a and 8b)	Revision of identity and culture (Modules 1, 4 and 7)
	Customs and traditions (Modules 7a and 7b)	Enterprise, employability and future plans (Modules 9a and 9b)	Revision of Wales and the world – areas of interest (Modules 2, 5 and 8)
Year 11	Revision of current and future study and employment (Modules 3, 6 and 9)	Revision of Wales and the world – areas of interest (Modules 2, 5 and 8)	Oral exam Revision
	Revision of identity and culture (Modules 1, 4 and 7)	Revision of current and future study and employment (Modules 3, 6 and 9)	

OVERVIEW OF TEXTBOOK CONTENT

YOUTH CULTURE: MODULE 1A

SELF AND RELATIONSHIPS (1)

Tasks	Contents	Grammar
Short reading	• Article on celebrity gossip • Choose the correct statements	• Present tense (*-er*, *-ir* and *-re* verbs) • Present tense (regular and irregular verbs)
Longer reading	• Newspaper article about personality • Q&A • **Extra**	
Listening	• Two young people talking about problems • **Assessed language task**: Choose the correct problem • **Extra**	
Speaking	• Photo card discussion	
Writing	• Short responses on four bullet points related to self and relationships • **Extra**	
Additional activities	• Translation into English	

YOUTH CULTURE: MODULE 1A

SELF AND RELATIONSHIPS (2)

Tasks	Contents	Grammar
Short reading	• Young people talking about their personality • **Assessed language task**: Choose the correct name	• Adjectives (position/ adjective endings/ irregular forms) • Asking questions (interrogatives)
Longer reading	• **Literary text**: Adapted from *Diam's Autobiographie* by Mélanie Georgides • Q&A	
Listening	• Monologue about family • Note key details	
Speaking	• Role play practice	
Writing	• Respond to four questions about yourself and your future plans	

YOUTH CULTURE: MODULE 1A

SELF AND RELATIONSHIPS (3)

Tasks	Contents	Grammar
Short reading	• Two young people talking about fashion • **Assessed language task**: Gap fill • **Extra**	• Possessive adjectives
Longer reading	• An article about a model • True/False	
Listening	• Interview with a French footballer • Q&A	
Speaking	• Conversation questions	
Writing	• Translation into French	

YOUTH CULTURE: MODULE 1B

TECHNOLOGY AND SOCIAL MEDIA (1)

Tasks	Contents	Grammar
Short reading	• Article about social media • Multiple choice	• Prepositions • **Extra**
Longer reading	• Article about mobile phones • Q&A • **Extra**	
Listening	• Monologue about podcasts • **Assessed language task**: Q&A	
Speaking	• Photo card discussion	
Writing	• Write an advert for a mobile/computer/tablet	
Additional activities	• Translation into English	

YOUTH CULTURE: MODULE 1B

TECHNOLOGY AND SOCIAL MEDIA (2)

Tasks	Contents	Grammar
Short reading	• **Literary text**: Adapted from *Manuel de survie pour les filles d'aujourd'hui* by Charlotte Grossetête • Q&A	• Negatives
Longer reading	• Article about Lily Rose Depp • **Assessed language task**: Gap fill	
Listening	• Report about a blogger • Q&A	
Speaking	• Role play practice	
Writing	• Write an article for your school website about social media • **Extra**	

YOUTH CULTURE: MODULE 1B

TECHNOLOGY AND SOCIAL MEDIA (3)

Tasks	Contents	Grammar
Short reading	• Statements about videogames • **Assessed language task**: Match the picture to the statement	• Future tense
Longer reading	• Article about 3D printers • Q&A	
Listening	• Report on a new invention • Note key details	
Speaking	• Conversation questions	
Writing	• Translation into French	

HOME AND LOCALITY: MODULE 2A

LOCAL AREAS OF INTEREST (1)

Tasks	Contents	Grammar
Short reading	• Four adverts for places in a town • **Assessed language task**: Match the advert to the statements	• *Je voudrais* • Imperfect tense
Longer reading	• Review of a local attraction • Q&A • **Extra**	
Listening	• Monologue about changes in the area • Make notes under headings	
Speaking	• Conversation questions	
Writing	• Write a paragraph about your area • **Extra**	

HOME AND LOCALITY: MODULE 2A

LOCAL AREAS OF INTEREST (2)

Tasks	Contents	Grammar
Short reading	• Advert for three towns • Note key details	• Imperative
Longer reading	• Reviews of attractions • Note key details	
Listening	• Description of a region • **Assessed language task**: Multiple choice questions	
Speaking	• Role play practice	
Writing	• Write an advert for an attraction in your area	
Additional activities	• Translation into English	

HOME AND LOCALITY: MODULE 2A

LOCAL AREAS OF INTEREST (3)

Tasks	Contents	Grammar
Short reading	• Four comments from young people about their local area • Match to the correct statements • **Extra**	• Conditional tense • *Venir de* • Formal letters
Longer reading	• Letter of complaint about a problem in a local area • **Assessed language task**: Q&A	
Listening	• News report about happiness with local area • Match statistics to the correct statements	
Speaking	• Photo card discussion	
Writing	• Translation into French	

HOME AND LOCALITY: MODULE 2B

TRAVEL AND TRANSPORT (1)

Tasks	Contents	Grammar
Short reading	• Four people talking about their journey to work • Note key details	• Comparative and superlative • Adjectives (position)
Longer reading	• Article about cycling to work • **Assessed language task**: Choose the correct statements • **Extra**	
Listening	• Ferry announcement • Q&A	
Speaking	• Conversation questions	
Writing	• Short responses on three bullet points about transport	

HOME AND LOCALITY: MODULE 2B

TRAVEL AND TRANSPORT (2)

Tasks	Contents	Grammar
Short reading	• Information on different tickets • **Assessed language task**: Match ticket to statement	• Adverbs • **Extra**
Longer reading	• Survey about transport • Q&A	
Listening	• Radio traffic report • Note key details	
Speaking	• Photo card discussion	
Writing	• Translation into French	
Additional activities	• Translation into English	

HOME AND LOCALITY: MODULE 2B

TRAVEL AND TRANSPORT (3)

Tasks	Contents	Grammar
Short reading	• Airport information • Gap fill • **Extra**	• Definite and indefinite articles
Longer reading	• **Literary text**: Extract from the novel *Elise ou la vraie vie* by Claire Etcherelli • Q&A	
Listening	• Conversation booking a ticket at a station • **Assessed language task**: Multiple choice	
Speaking	• Role play practice	
Writing	• Write a blog about a journey	

CURRENT STUDY: MODULE 3A

SCHOOL/COLLEGE LIFE (1)

Tasks	Contents	Grammar
Short reading	• Information on school subjects • **Assessed language task**: Q&A	• Perfect tense with *avoir*
Longer reading	• **Literary text**: Extract from the novel *Coup de Foudre au collège* by Louise Leroi • Q&A	
Listening	• Conversation about school • Choose the correct statements	
Speaking	• Photo card discussion	
Writing	• Short response on six bullet points about school	

CURRENT STUDY: MODULE 3A

SCHOOL/COLLEGE LIFE (2)

Tasks	Contents	Grammar
Short reading	• School rules • Match up to the English	• Perfect tense with *être*
Longer reading	• Social media posts about school • **Assessed language task**: Q&A • **Extra**	
Listening	• Conversation about school subjects • Q&A	
Speaking	• Role play practice	
Writing	• Write a reply to an e-mail about school • **Extra**	
Additional activities	• Translation into English	

CURRENT STUDY: MODULE 3A

SCHOOL/COLLEGE LIFE (3)

Tasks	Contents	Grammar
Short reading	• School web page • Q&A	• Time and numbers
Longer reading	• Text about teachers • Gap fill	
Listening	• Statements about French and British schools • **Assessed language task**: Decide if the statements refer to French or British schools	
Speaking	• Conversation questions	
Writing	• Translation into French	

CURRENT STUDY: MODULE 3B

SCHOOL/COLLEGE STUDIES (1)

Tasks	Contents	Grammar
Short reading	• Opinions on school subjects • **Assessed language task**: Match to the correct picture • **Extra**	• Indefinite adjectives
Longer reading	• Subject option guide for a *lycée* • Note key information	
Listening	• Conversation about *le lycée* • Q&A	
Speaking	• Role play practice	
Writing	• Write an article about school • **Extra**	

CURRENT STUDY: MODULE 3B

SCHOOL/COLLEGE STUDIES (2)

Tasks	Contents	Grammar
Short reading	• **Literary text**: Extract from Mylène Farmer's biography • Q&A	• Personal pronouns
Longer reading	• School problems and advice • Note key details	
Listening	• Teacher talking about school • **Assessed language task**: Multiple choice questions	
Speaking	• Conversation questions	
Writing	• Translation into French	
Additional activities	• Translation into English	

CURRENT STUDY: MODULE 3B

SCHOOL/COLLEGE STUDIES (3)

Tasks	Contents	Grammar
Short reading	• Comments about school related stress/problems • Find the French • **Extra**	• Object pronouns
Longer reading	• Article about exam stress • Gap fill	
Listening	• Advice for exams • **Assessed language task**: Q&A	
Speaking	• Photo card discussion	
Writing	• Write an e-mail to your friend about school life	

LIFESTYLE: MODULE 4A

HEALTH AND FITNESS (1)

Tasks	Contents	Grammar
Short reading	• Four people talking about health • **Assessed language task**: Choose the correct person • **Extra**	• Demonstrative adjectives
Longer reading	• Information on healthy lunchtime choices • Choose the correct statements	
Listening	• News report on eating habits • Q&A	
Speaking	• Photo card discussion	
Writing	• Give short responses on four bullet points about food	

LIFESTYLE: MODULE 4A

HEALTH AND FITNESS (2)

Tasks	Contents	Grammar
Short reading	• **Literary text**: Questionnaire from the diet book *Le nouveau régime* • Q&A	• Present tense reflexive verbs
Longer reading	• Information on a French footballer • **Assessed language task**: Gap fill	
Listening	• Advert for a tennis club • Q&A	
Speaking	• Role play practice	
Writing	• Translation into French	

LIFESTYLE: MODULE 4A

HEALTH AND FITNESS (3)

Tasks	Contents	Grammar
Short reading	• News article on alcohol • Gap fill	• Relative pronouns
Longer reading	• News article on young people and alcohol • Choose the false statements • **Extra**	
Listening	• Report on health of French people • **Assessed language task**: Q&A	
Speaking	• Conversation questions	
Writing	• Write an article on young people and health	
Additional activities	• Translation into English	

LIFESTYLE: MODULE 4B

ENTERTAINMENT AND LEISURE (1)

Tasks	Contents	Grammar
Short reading	• Four people talking about videogames • Choose the correct person for each statement	• Conjunctions
Longer reading	• Film review • Note key details	
Listening	• Interview with a videogame addict • **Assessed language task**: Q&A	
Speaking	• Photo card discussion	
Writing	• Short responses on five bullet points on entertainment and leisure • **Extra**	

LIFESTYLE: MODULE 4B

ENTERTAINMENT AND LEISURE (2)

Tasks	Contents	Grammar
Short reading	• Magazine quiz about shopping • **Assessed language task**: Match to the correct statements	• Present participle
Longer reading	• Information on restaurants • Note key details	
Listening	• Voice-mail left for a friend • Gap fill	
Speaking	• Role play practice	
Writing	• Translation into French	
Additional activities	• Translation into English	

LIFESTYLE: MODULE 4B

ENTERTAINMENT AND LEISURE (3)

Tasks	Contents	Grammar
Short reading	• **Literary text**: Extract from the short story *Max et Ninon* by Lilias Nord • Q&A	• Tenses with *si*
Longer reading	• Article on free time • **Assessed language task**: Choose correct statements • **Extra**	
Listening	• Radio article about a new music group • Q&A	
Speaking	• Conversation questions	
Writing	• Write an e-mail to your friend about your hobbies	

THE WIDER WORLD: MODULE 5A

LOCAL AND REGIONAL FEATURES AND CHARCTERISTICS OF FRANCE AND FRENCH-SPEAKING COUNTRIES (1)

Tasks	Contents	Grammar
Short reading	• Article on Mauritius • **Assessed language task**: Q&A	• Weather verbs
Longer reading	• Tourist information advert about Quebec • Choose the correct statements • **Extra**	
Listening	• Information on excursions • Note key details	
Speaking	• Conversation questions	
Writing	• Write a paragraph on a country you have visited	

THE WIDER WORLD: MODULE 5A

LOCAL AND REGIONAL FEATURES AND CHARCTERISTICS OF FRANCE AND FRENCH-SPEAKING COUNTRIES (2)

Tasks	Contents	Grammar
Short reading	• Factual information on four French tourist attractions • Choose the correct attraction for each statement • **Extra**	• Verbs followed by prepositions
Longer reading	• **Literary text**: Extract from the novel *Eugénie Grandet* by Honoré de Balzac • Q&A	
Listening	• Report on Strasbourg • **Assessed language task**: Multiple choice questions	
Speaking	• Photo card discussion	
Writing	• An article on a tourist attraction you would like to visit	
Additional activities	• Translation into English	

THE WIDER WORLD: MODULE 5A

LOCAL AND REGIONAL FEATURES AND CHARCTERISTICS OF FRANCE AND FRENCH-SPEAKING COUNTRIES (3)

Tasks	Contents	Grammar
Short reading	• Information about the town of Calvi in Corsica • Q&A	• Subjunctive
Longer reading	• Leaflet about Château de Vayres • **Assessed language task**: Choose the correct statements • **Extra**	
Listening	• Announcement for Stade de France • Q&A	
Speaking	• Role play practice	
Writing	• Translation into French	

THE WIDER WORLD: MODULE 5B

HOLIDAYS AND TOURISM (1)

Tasks	Contents	Grammar
Short reading	• Information about four hotels • **Assessed language task**: Choose the correct hotel	• Reminder: past/present/future
Longer reading	• TripAdvisor style review of a hotel • Note key details	
Listening	• Two people discussing holidays • Q&A	
Speaking	• Role play practice	
Writing	• Short responses on six bullet points about a past holiday	

THE WIDER WORLD: MODULE 5B

HOLIDAYS AND TOURISM (2)

Tasks	Contents	Grammar
Short reading	• Six statements about holidays • Choose the correct person	• Pluperfect tense
Longer reading	• E-mail booking a hotel • **Assessed language task**: Multiple choice questions	
Listening	• Advert for a competition to win a holiday • Note key information	
Speaking	• Conversation questions	
Writing	• Write an article on young people and holidays	
Additional activities	• Translation into English	

THE WIDER WORLD: MODULE 5B

HOLIDAYS AND TOURISM (3)

Tasks	Contents	Grammar
Short reading	• Article on visitors to the town of Vannes • Q&A	• Formal e-mails
Longer reading	• **Literary text**: Extract from the novel *Vendredi ou la vie sauvage* by Michel Tournier • Q&A	
Listening	• Report on a holiday camp • **Assessed language task**: Q&A	
Speaking	• Photo card discussion	
Writing	• Translation into French	

ENTERPRISE, EMPLOYABILITY AND FUTURE PLANS: MODULE 6A

EMPLOYMENT (1)

Tasks	Contents	Grammar
Short reading	• Young people talking about first jobs • Note key points	• Perfect infinitive
Longer reading	• Article about an unusual job • **Assessed language task**: Choose the correct statements	
Listening	• Survey about young people and money • Choose the correct statements	
Speaking	• Conversation questions	
Writing	• Write three advantages and three disadvantages of holiday work	

ENTERPRISE, EMPLOYABILITY AND FUTURE PLANS: MODULE 6A

EMPLOYMENT (2)

Tasks	Contents	Grammar
Short reading	• **Literary text**: Extract from the novel *L'Étranger* by Albert Camus • Q&A	• *Depuis*
Longer reading	• How young people earn money • Note key points	
Listening	• Account of a holiday job • **Assessed language task**: Gap fill	
Speaking	• Photo card discussion	
Writing	• Translation into French	

ENTERPRISE, EMPLOYABILITY AND FUTURE PLANS: MODULE 6A

EMPLOYMENT (3)

Tasks	Contents	Grammar
Short reading	• Young people talking about holiday jobs • **Assessed language task**: Match the statements to the correct job	• Emphatic pronouns
Longer reading	• Article about voluntary work • Q&A	
Listening	• Monologue about a summer job • Q&A	
Speaking	• Role play practice	
Writing	• Write a job application letter applying for a summer job	
Additional activities	• Translation into English	

ENTERPRISE, EMPLOYABILITY AND FUTURE PLANS: MODULE 6B

SKILLS AND PERSONAL QUALITIES (1)

Tasks	Contents	Grammar
Short reading	• Blog about career plans • Q&A	• Indirect object pronouns
Longer reading	• **Literary text**: Extract from the novel *Enzo, 11 ans sixième 11* by Joëlle Ecormier • Q&A • **Extra**	
Listening	• Interview with a hotel boss • **Assessed language task**: Choose correct statement	
Speaking	• Role play practice	
Writing	• Translation into French	

ENTERPRISE, EMPLOYABILITY AND FUTURE PLANS: MODULE 6B

SKILLS AND PERSONAL QUALITIES (2)

Tasks	Contents	Grammar
Short reading	• People talking about their work preferences • **Assessed language task**: Match to job option	• Demonstrative pronouns
Longer reading	• Article on different personality types • Match the correct statement	
Listening	• Report about the importance of learning languages • Q&A	
Speaking	• Photo card discussion	
Writing	• Short responses for five jobs explaining the skills and personal qualities that are needed for each one	
Additional activities	• Translation into English	

ENTERPRISE, EMPLOYABILITY AND FUTURE PLANS: MODULE 6B

SKILLS AND PERSONAL QUALITIES (3)

Tasks	Contents	Grammar
Short reading	• Top 10 qualities employers are looking for • Match to the English	• Possessive pronouns
Longer reading	• Article on preparation for the world of work • **Assessed language task**: Gap fill • **Extra**	
Listening	• Advert for a course • Q&A	
Speaking	• Conversation questions	
Writing	• Write a paragraph on your skills and personal qualities • **Extra**	

CUSTOMS AND TRADITIONS: MODULE 7A

FOOD AND DRINK (1)

Tasks	Contents	Grammar
Short reading	• Opinions on food • Match the halves • **Extra**	• Adverbs: quantifiers and intensifiers
Longer reading	• Article on 'la raclette' • Q&A	
Listening	• Interview with a baker • **Assessed language task**: Multiple choice questions	
Speaking	• Conversation questions	
Writing	• Write an article about typical/traditional foods	

CUSTOMS AND TRADITIONS: MODULE 7A

FOOD AND DRINK (2)

Tasks	Contents	Grammar
Short reading	• Information from restaurant websites • **Assessed language task**: Match the restaurants	• Adverbs of place and time
Longer reading	• TripAdvisor style restaurant review • Note key points	
Listening	• Complaint in a restaurant • Q&A	
Speaking	• Role play practice	
Writing	• Write a restaurant review • **Extra**	
Additional activities	• Translation into English	

CUSTOMS AND TRADITIONS: MODULE 7A

FOOD AND DRINK (3)

Tasks	Contents	Grammar
Short reading	• Article on couscous • Q&A	• Expression of quantities using *de*
Longer reading	• **Literary text**: Extract from the book *Petits Gâteaux de Grands Pâtissiers* by Cécile Coulier • **Assessed language task**: Multiple choice questions	
Listening	• Report on family mealtimes • Q&A	
Speaking	• Photo card discussion	
Writing	• Translation into French	

CUSTOMS AND TRADITIONS: MODULE 7B

FESTIVALS AND CELEBRATIONS (1)

Tasks	Contents	Grammar
Short reading	• Announcement for a baby's birth • Q&A	• Adverbs: comparative and superlative
Longer reading	• How people celebrate their birthday • **Assessed language task**: Choose the correct person • **Extra**	
Listening	• Conversation about a party • Q&A	
Speaking	• Photo card discussion	
Writing	• Short responses on five bullet points about parties/ birthdays	

CUSTOMS AND TRADITIONS: MODULE 7B

FESTIVALS AND CELEBRATIONS (2)

Tasks	Contents	Grammar
Short reading	• Ten things you need for a festival • Match to the English	• Perfect tense with reflexive verbs
Longer reading	• Advert for a festival • Q&A	
Listening	• Advert for a festival • **Assessed language task**: Note key points	
Speaking	• Role play practice	
Writing	• Write an article for a music magazine about festivals	
Additional activities	• Translation into English	

CUSTOMS AND TRADITIONS: MODULE 7B

FESTIVALS AND CELEBRATIONS (3)

Tasks	Contents	Grammar
Short reading	• Article about Cannes Film Festival • **Assessed language task**: Gap fill	• *En, au, aux*
Longer reading	• **Literary text**: Extract from the novel *Le mort au Festival de Cannes* by Brigitte Aubert • Q&A	
Listening	• Report on a festival • Q&A	
Speaking	• Conversation questions	
Writing	• Translation into French	
Additional activities	• Translation into English	

GLOBAL SUSTAINABILITY: MODULE 8A

ENVIRONMENT (1)

Tasks	Contents	Grammar
Short reading	• Ten environmental problems • Match to the English	• Indefinite pronouns
Longer reading	• **Literary text**: Extract from the poem 'L'environnement' by Mariche Ahcene • Q&A	
Listening	• Report on environmental problems • **Assessed language task**: Gap fill	
Speaking	• Role play practice	
Writing	• Short responses about bullet points on the environment	
Additional activities	• Translation into English	

GLOBAL SUSTAINABILITY: MODULE 8A

ENVIRONMENT (2)

Tasks	Contents	Grammar
Short reading	• Information on recycling • Note key details	• The passive
Longer reading	• Magazine article about making models from recycling • **Assessed language task**: Gap fill	
Listening	• Report on how long items take to decompose • Note key points	
Speaking	• Photo card discussion	
Writing	• Write an advert on the importance of recycling	

GLOBAL SUSTAINABILITY: MODULE 8A

ENVIRONMENT (3)

Tasks	Contents	Grammar
Short reading	• Statements about renewable energy • **Assessed language task**: Gap fill	• *Depuis*
Longer reading	• Article about renewable energy • Choose the correct statements	
Listening	• News report on the environment • Q&A	
Speaking	• Conversation questions	
Writing	• Translation into French	

GLOBAL SUSTAINABILITY: MODULE 8B

SOCIAL ISSUES (1)

Tasks	Contents	Grammar
Short reading	• Statements about poverty in France • **Assessed language task**: Match the statements	• Planning an extended written response
Longer reading	• Article on homelessness in France • Q&A	
Listening	• News report on an epidemic • Q&A	
Speaking	• Photo card discussion	
Writing	• Write a formal letter to the government about a social issue that concerns you	
Additional activities	• Translation into English	

GLOBAL SUSTAINABILITY: MODULE 8B

SOCIAL ISSUES (2)

Tasks	Contents	Grammar
Short reading	• Survey about immigration • Gap fill	• Numbers
Longer reading	• **Literary text**: Extract from the novel *La fabrique du monstre : 10 ans d'immersion dans les quartiers nord de Marseille, la zone la plus pauvre d'Europe* by Philippe Pujol • Q&A	
Listening	• Radio report on a charity event • **Assessed language task**: Choose the correct statements • **Extra**	
Speaking	• Conversation questions	
Writing	• Translation into French	

GLOBAL SUSTAINABILITY: MODULE 8B

SOCIAL ISSUES (3)

Tasks	Contents	Grammar
Short reading	• Advert for UNICEF • Q&A	• Planning detailed responses on social issues
Longer reading	• Information on a charity event • **Assessed language task**: Multiple choice questions	
Listening	• Two people talking about raising money • Q&A	
Speaking	• Role play practice	
Writing	• Write an advert for a charity event you are organising	

ENTERPRISE, EMPLOYABILITY AND FUTURE PLANS: MODULE 9A

POST-16 STUDY (1)

Tasks	Contents	Grammar
Short reading	• Advice about creating a CV • Match to the correct statements	• Useful expressions
Longer reading	• Newspaper article on a job forum • Note key details	
Listening	• Six young people talking about future plans • **Assessed language task**: Choose a job for them and give a reason	
Speaking	• Photo card discussion	
Writing	• Write a letter applying for a job	

ENTERPRISE, EMPLOYABILITY AND FUTURE PLANS: MODULE 9A

POST-16 STUDY (2)

Tasks	Contents	Grammar
Short reading	• Information about a BTS school • **Assessed language task**: Choose the correct course • **Extra**	• Expressing opinions
Longer reading	• **Literary text**: Extract from the novel *Stupeur et tremblements* by Amélie Nothomb • Q&A	
Listening	• Information on a course • Q&A	
Speaking	• Conversation questions	
Writing	• Translation into French	
Additional activities	• Translation into English	

ENTERPRISE, EMPLOYABILITY AND FUTURE PLANS: MODULE 9A

POST-16 STUDY (3)

Tasks	Contents	Grammar
Short reading	• Interview questions • Match to the English	• Illustrating points
Longer reading	• Article on interviews • **Assessed language task**: Gap fill	
Listening	• Interview for a part-time job • Q&A	
Speaking	• Role play practice	
Writing	• Answer three interview questions	

ENTERPRISE, EMPLOYABILITY AND FUTURE PLANS: MODULE 9B

CAREER PLANS (1)

Tasks	Contents	Grammar
Short reading	• Statements about work and university • **Assessed language task**: Decide if the statements relate to work, university or both • **Extra**	• Emphasising points • Letters of application
Longer reading	• Article about studying abroad • Q&A	
Listening	• Advert for a course • Q&A	
Speaking	• Photo card discussion	
Writing	• Write a letter to participate in a study programme abroad	

ENTERPRISE, EMPLOYABILITY AND FUTURE PLANS: MODULE 9B

CAREER PLANS (2)

Tasks	Contents	Grammar
Short reading	• Survey about young people and work • Choose the correct percentage for each statement	• *Pendant* – for/during
Longer reading	• Article on foreign students working in France • **Assessed language task**: Choose the correct statements	
Listening	• Report about being an au pair • Q&A	
Speaking	• Conversation questions	
Writing	• Translation into French	

ENTERPRISE, EMPLOYABILITY AND FUTURE PLANS: MODULE 9B

CAREER PLANS (3)

Tasks	Contents	Grammar
Short reading	• Six young people saying what they would like to do in the future • Choose the correct person	• Future plan phrases
Longer reading	• **Literary text**: Extract from the novel *Désolée, je suis attendue* by Agnès Martin-Lugand • Q&A	
Listening	• Young people talking about future plans • **Assessed language task**: Choose the correct person	
Speaking	• Role play practice	
Writing	• Write a paragraph about your future plans	
Additional activities	• Translation into English	

OVERVIEW FOR GRAMMAR IN CONTEXT

	Identity and culture	Wales and the world – areas of interest	Current and future study and employment
Unit 1 Modules 1–3	**Youth culture (1a and 1b)** 1. Present tense 2. Word order 3. Asking questions 4. Possessive adjectives 5. Future tense 6. Immediate future	**Home and locality (2a and 2b)** 1. Imperfect tense 2. Commands 3. Conditional 4. Adjectives: comparatives and superlatives 5. Adverbs 6. Present tense	**Current study (3a and 3b)** 1. The perfect tense with *avoir* 2. The perfect tense with *être* 3. *Être* or *avoir*? 4. The time 5. Indefinite adjectives 6. Object pronouns
Unit 2 Modules 4–6	**Lifestyle (4a and 4b)** 1. Demonstrative adjectives 2. Present tense reflexive verbs 3. Relative pronouns 4. Conjunctions 5. The present participle 6. Tenses with *si*	**The wider world (5a and 5b)** 1. Weather verbs 2. Verbs followed by prepositions 3. The subjunctive 4. Taking about a holiday in the past, present and future 5. Using different tenses to talk about holidays 6. Pluperfect tense	**Enterprise, employability and future plans (6a and 6b)** 1. Perfect infinitive 2. *Depuis* 3. Emphatic pronouns 4. Indirect object pronouns 5. Demonstrative pronouns 6. Possessive pronouns
Unit 3 Modules 7–9	**Customs and traditions (7a and 7b)** 1. Adverbs: quantifiers and intensifiers 2. Adverbs of place and time 3. Expressions of quantities using *de* 4. Adverbs: comparatives and superlatives 5. Perfect tense with reflexive verbs 6. *En, au, aux, à la*	**Global sustainability (8a and 8b)** 1. Indefinite pronouns 2. The passive 3. *Depuis* 4. Useful verbs 5. Revising tenses 6. Using a variety of adjectives	**Enterprise, employability and future plans (9a and 9b)** 1. Talking about the future in different ways 2. Basic accuracy 3. Illustrating points and expressing opinions 4. Writing a letter of application 5. *Pendant* – for/during 6. Revising your tenses

TRANSCRIPTS AND ANSWERS

THEME: IDENTITY AND CULTURE

UNIT 1

YOUTH CULTURE

1A SELF AND RELATIONSHIPS (1)

READING

Answers:

The correct statements are 2, 4, 5, 8, 10

READING

Suggested translations:

1. My best friend is funny, nice and understanding.
2. My sister has lots of friends.
3. I get on well with my parents.
4. What qualities does a good friend have?

READING

Answers:

1. Wants to change/be someone different/ change his look/image
2. Shy/timid, boring
3. At the end of secondary school
4. He wants to follow the crowd/he wants to stand out/be individual
5. To wear clothes he likes
6. Will reassure him/give him confidence

EXTRA

Extra – Suggested translations:

je suis timide, ennuyeux
I am shy, boring

mais j'ai aussi peur !
But I am also frightened!

tu n'es pas seul
You are not alone

L'important, c'est que tu portes des vêtements que tu aimes
The important thing is that you wear clothes that you like

LISTENING

Transcript:

Interviewer : Vous êtes stressée dans la vie Madame ?

Charlotte : Oui, bien sûr, je suis stressée par le travail et aussi parce que j'ai des problèmes familiaux.

Interviewer : Et vous, Monsieur ?

Benjamin : Tout me stresse, par exemple, les amis et mes parents.

Answers:

	Métier	Famille	Amis
Charlotte	✓	✓	
Benjamin		✓	✓

EXTRA

Extra

1. parce que j'ai des problèmes
2. tout me stresse

1A SELF AND RELATIONSHIPS (2)

READING

Answers:

1. Eric
2. Sylvie
3. Luc
4. Sylvie
5. Luc
6. Arnaud

READING

Answers:

1. 25 July 1980
2. Her mother had married a man from Cyprus/living in Cyprus
3. Proud
4. Her name
5. Singer
6. It was his mother's name

LISTENING

Transcript:

Je m'appelle Clara. Alors, je suis grande et maigre. J'ai les yeux bruns et les cheveux longs, raides et châtains.

Une des filles de ma classe dit que je suis triste et calme, mais ce n'est pas vrai. Je suis contente et bavarde.

Mon père s'appelle Yves, il est comptable. Il donne l'impression d'être intelligent et sérieux, mais en fait il est très bête et pénible. Mais je m'entends bien avec mon père. Il est grand et gros. Il a les yeux marron comme moi.

Ma mère s'appelle Maude, elle reste à la maison. Elle est bête et bavarde. Elle a les yeux verts. Je trouve que ma mère est belle.

Mon frère s'appelle Guillaume et il a cinq ans. Il est pénible. Il est petit et laid. Il a les yeux bleus et les cheveux châtains, courts et raides. Il aime le football et les dinosaures. Je déteste mon frère parce qu'il ne me laisse pas tranquille !

Answers:

Clara

Tall/big, thin, brown eyes, long straight brown hair. She is happy and chatty.

Yves

Tall/big, fat, brown eyes. He is silly and annoying.

Maude

Green eyes, pretty. She is silly and chatty.

Guillaume

Small, ugly, blue eyes. Short, straight brown hair. He is annoying.

1A SELF AND RELATIONSHIPS (3)

READING

Answers:

1. magazines
2. passion
3. ville
4. actrices
5. grandes
6. dernier
7. sont
8. dois

EXTRA

Extra:

1. Tout ce dont j'ai besoin
2. Je dois faire attention
3. J'adore suivre
4. Il faut
5. Je m'inspire

READING

Answers:

1. True
2. False
3. True
4. False
5. False
6. False

LISTENING

Transcript:

Interviewer : Bafétimbi Gomis, vous êtes joueur de football pour l'équipe de France et vous jouez en Premier League au Royaume-Uni. Aujourd'hui, nous avons l'occasion de parler de votre vie. Voulez-vous nous parler de votre enfance ?

Gomis : Je suis né en France mais mes parents sont d'origine sénégalaise. Je suis né le six août mille neuf cent quatre-vingt-cinq. J'ai grandi dans une banlieue de Toulon. À l'âge de quinze ans, j'ai commencé à jouer dans le championnat professionnel en France.

Interviewer : Parlez-moi de votre vie privée.

Gomis : Je suis très content parce que je viens d'être papa pour la deuxième fois. On a baptisé ma deuxième fille Yzatis. Elle ressemble à une petite princesse. On a annoncé l'heureux événement sur les réseaux sociaux. Je voudrais toutes et tous vous remercier pour vos nombreux messages de félicitations, qui me vont droit au cœur.

Answers:

1. 6 August 1985
2. Suburbs/outskirts
3. Began playing football in France in the Championship/playing professional football
4. Birth/arrival of his daughter/new baby/just become a dad for second time
5. Messages of congratulations

WRITING

Suggested translations:

1. Karl est l'ami de sa mère.
2. Isabelle est mannequin depuis juillet dernier.
3. Isabelle est mannequin de lunettes de soleil.
4. Karl la connatt depuis la moitié de sa vie.

1B TECHNOLOGY AND SOCIAL MEDIA (1)

READING

Answers:

1. a, b
2. c
3. b, c
4. a
5. a

READING

Answers:

1. Contact friends, independence
2. Send SMS (texts), use social networks, talk to friends
3. 80
4. 68%

EXTRA

Extra – Suggested translations:

Un portable permet aux jeunes de se connecter avec leurs amis
A mobile phone allows young people to link up with friends

C'est pourquoi
That is why

Les jeunes font des échanges
Young people exchange

les réseaux sociaux
social networks

leurs meilleurs amis
their best friends

construire des liens sociaux
build social networks

plusieurs fois par jour
several times a day

READING

Answers:

1. Technology is very important in my life.
2. My mother doesn't use social media.
3. Young people spend too much time on their mobiles.
4. I would like a new computer.

GRAMMAR

EXTRA

Answers:

avant le dîner
before dinner

Je l'ai déjà vu
I have already seen it

à la mode
in fashion

dans un magasin
in a shop

à gauche
on the left

sur les réseaux sociaux
on social network sites

LISTENING

Transcript:

J'ai commencé à faire un podcast sur ma famille et mes amis. Les podcasts offrent un nouveau moyen d'enregistrer les devoirs, et j'enregistrerai mes devoirs de sport sur un podcast ce soir.

Ma mère dit que tout change à l'école et elle n'est pas convaincue que la technologie aide les jeunes à apprendre.

Mes amis et moi utilisons l'ordinateur pour nos études, tous les jours. À mon avis, la technologie est utile est rapide.

Answers:

1. Famille, amis
2. Devoirs de sport
3. Tout change à l'école, la technologie n'aide pas les jeunes à apprendre
4. Utile, rapide

1B TECHNOLOGY AND SOCIAL MEDIA (2)

READING

Answers:

1. Computer won't switch on
2. Three days
3. Reformat it and get advice from everyone
4. Cross
5. Hit the computer
6. Take it to be repaired

READING

Answers:

1. facile
2. jours
3. idée
4. a
5. quand
6. gens
7. frère
8. ennuyeux

LISTENING

Transcript:

Marie Lopez, idole des jeunes, est une star du web connue sous le pseudonyme « EnjoyPhoenix ». Son livre est en tête des ventes. Depuis deux mille onze, elle poste sur YouTube des tutoriels sur le maquillage et la mode. Elle fait des vlogs vidéos dans lesquelles elle filme sa vie quotidienne.

Suivie par plus d'un million virgule six abonnés, la jeune fille du sud-ouest de la France, qui n'a que vingt ans, gagnerait près de trois cent mille euros chaque année !

Answers:

1. A book
2. 2011
3. Make-up and fashion
4. Her daily life/her daily routine
5. 1.6 million
6. South-west France
7. 20 years
8. €300,000 a year

1B TECHNOLOGY AND SOCIAL MEDIA (3)

LISTENING

Transcript:

C'est peut-être la voiture de demain ! Il y a quelques semaines, Google a présenté son deuxième modèle de voiture autonome. Ça veut dire une voiture qui roule seule, sans humain. L'entreprise a placé des caméras et des radars sur le véhicule. Ils servent à détecter la présence d'obstacles sur la route et à se guider. La voiture peut se garer toute seule !

En cas d'urgence, le passager doit appuyer sur un bouton rouge pour tout arrêter.

Sa vitesse sera limitée à quarante kilomètres par heure et elle ne roulera qu'en ville.

Answers:

- Product: car that drives itself
- Features: cameras, radar
- Safety features: can detect obstacles, there is a red emergency stop button
- Limitations: maximum speed 40km/h, can only be used in town

READING

Answers:

1. d
2. c
3. b
4. g
5. f

READING

Answers:

1. Clothes: T-shirts, skirts, dresses
2. Printer
3. Three
4. One year
5. USA
6. Sell them
7. Blue, white, pink

WRITING

Suggested translations:

1. Les jeunes sont toujours sur leurs portables.
2. Ma mère a un vieil ordinateur.
3. Mon portable ne marche plus.
4. La technologie sera différente à l'avenir.
5. Je voudrais acheter une nouvelle tablette.

1A SELF AND RELATIONSHIPS

1B TECHNOLOGY AND SOCIAL MEDIA

GRAMMAR IN CONTEXT

GRAMMAR

1. PRESENT TENSE

1. Je chante au concert avec mes amis.
2. Tu finis tes devoirs.
3. Tu choisis tes propres vêtements.
4. J'ai un bon style !

2. WORD ORDER

1. Les chanteuses sont très belles.
2. J'ai un vieux portable !
3. Je m'entends bien avec mes parents, ils sont sympas.
4. Annie est vraiment heureuse.

3. ASKING QUESTIONS

1. Are you going to the concert?
2. What are you doing tonight?
3. What time are you going to the cinema?

Suggested questions:

Tu vas au concert quand ?

Où est-ce que tu vas ce soir ?

Comment est-ce que tu vas au concert ?

Pourquoi vas-tu au concert ce soir ?

Quand vas-tu au concert ?

4. POSSESSIVE ADJECTIVES

1. Ma tante habite en France.
2. Ton portable est super.
3. Je m'entends bien avec mon père.
4. Mes parents aiment aller au cinéma.
5. Nos amis sont très importants.
6. Combien de temps passes-tu sur ton ordinateur ?

5. FUTURE TENSE

1. c
2. a
3. b
4. d

6. IMMEDIATE FUTURE

1. Je vais acheter un ordinateur.
2. Il va voir sa famille.
3. Nous allons manger dans un restaurant.
4. Elle va lire un blog.
5. Je vais envoyer un e-mail.

THEME: WALES AND THE WORLD – AREAS OF INTEREST

UNIT 1

HOME AND LOCALITY

2A LOCAL AREAS OF INTEREST (1)

READING

Answers:

1. B
2. A
3. A
4. D
5. C
6. B

READING

Answers:

1. incredible, unbelievable
2. water, good for health
3. disgusting
4. bakers
5. eat raisin cakes
6. spring – not too hot and not too many tourists

LISTENING

Transcript:

Gaëlle : J'habite dans une ville dans le Nord. Elle est près des montagnes et c'est une vieille ville.

J'y habite depuis trois ans. Autrefois, j'habitais dans un village. Le village se trouvait à la campagne, pas loin d'une ferme. C'était une région rurale. Là-bas il n'y avait pas de cinéma et il y avait très peu de magasins. C'était ennuyeux. Il n'y avait qu'une piscine.

Je préfère habiter en ville parce qu'il y a plus de distractions et j'aime aller en boîte avec mes amis.

Dans le passé, les alentours de la ville étaient très industrialisés. Il y avait des mines de charbon pas loin de la ville. Cependant, les villages étaient très agricoles. Aujourd'hui les deux régions sont touristiques.

Answers:

	Where she lives now	Where she used to live
Details about region	Town Mountains Historic	Village Countryside Farm
Things to do and see	Nightclub	Swimming pool
Her preferences and reasons why	Town More entertainment, things to do	
What the area was like in the past	Industrial (coal mines)	Agricultural/rural
What the area is like today	Good for tourists	Good for tourists

2A LOCAL AREAS OF INTEREST (2)

READING

Answers:

Brest: charming garden, abbey ruins, the port

Saint-Brieuc: bay, sport, beach

Le Trégor: cathedral, churches, castle, garden

EXTRA

Extra

était – was

Il y avait – there was

On disait – it was said

READING

Answers:

	Review 1	Review 2	Review 3	Review 4
Date of review	17 June	1 February	29 August	July
Opinion	Beautiful	Wonderful scenery	Magnificent	Beautiful beach
Other details	Theme park outdated	In winter not many visitors, quiet. Use the steps instead of chairlift. It is cheaper, good for your health and mind	Pay £4.50 to park for the whole day	Chairlift will take you down. A little expensive and costs £6

LISTENING

Transcript:

Marie-Christine : J'adore mon village. Il se trouve au bord de la mer dans une région touristique. Il y a beaucoup de choses à faire si on s'intéresse aux sports nautiques.

Le samedi, je sors avec mes copains. Nous allons à la plage et on fait de la planche à voile.

Après ça, on rentre à la maison qui se trouve à cinq kilomètres du centre du village. En été, on mange dans le jardin.

Answers:

1. b
2. a
3. b
4. c
5. a

READING

Suggested translations:

1. The theme park is great but expensive.
2. I would like to visit the stadium.
3. I like my town but there are too many tourists.
4. The village is located at the seaside.

2A LOCAL AREAS OF INTEREST (3)

READING

Answers:

1. Nicole
2. Simon
3. André
4. Nicole
5. Louise
6. Simon

EXTRA

Extra – Suggested translations:

J'aimerais avoir une piscine
I would like to have a swimming pool

Il y a trop de pollution à cause des voitures
There is too much pollution because of the cars

Je voudrais habiter au bord de la mer
I would like to live by the sea

Il n'y a pas de grands magasins
There aren't any big shops

Il y a des avantages comme les parcs d'attraction
There are benefits such as theme parks

WRITING

Suggested translation:

J'aime habiter dans ma ville parce qu'il y a beaucoup de magasins et restaurants. Il y avait un cinéma mais maintenant il y a un centre commercial. Je voudrais habiter en France parce que j'aime la cuisine française.

LISTENING

Transcript:

La Commission européenne vient de publier les conclusions d'un sondage réalisé parmi quatre-vingts grandes villes européennes, pour mesurer le niveau de satisfaction de leurs habitants.

Il conclut que quatre-vingts pourcent des habitants de Marseille sont heureux d'habiter dans la ville.

Il y a trois ans qu'un sondage a conclu que soixante-quinze pourcent des habitants de Marseille sont heureux d'y habiter. Il y a un accroissement de cinq pourcent cette année.

Le sondage a noté que seize pourcent des habitants de Marseille se sentent en sécurité dans la ville.

Answers:

1. 80
2. 80%
3. Three years
4. 75%
5. 5%
6. 16%

READING

Answers:

1. Appartement
2. Appartement en face
3. Le weekend
4. Bruit, musique, fêtes
5. Porter plainte à la mairie
6. La fatigue/le bruit

2B TRAVEL AND TRANSPORT (1)

READING

Answers:

Jean-Claude
Transport to work: train
Reason: not got a car
Other details given: it's practical

Marie-Thèrèse
Transport to work: bus
Reason: faster than walking
Other details given: works in morning

Suzanne
Transport to work: car
Reason: she has her own car
Other details given: it's expensive

Daniel
Transport to work: walks
Reason: works opposite his house
Other details given: works in office

READING

Answers:

2, 3, 7, 8, 9, 10

EXTRA

Translate the four incorrect sentences into English.

Answers :

1. One can have a free bike before the New Year.
4. The bikes will be old.
5. The company Orange has already bought a lot of bikes.
6. The government helps employees to buy their own bike.

LISTENING

Transcript:

Nous sommes heureux de vous accueillir à bord du Pont Aven. Le bureau des informations se trouve en face du restaurant.

L'accès au garage est strictement interdit pendant le voyage.

En cas de mauvais temps, il est interdit de sortir dehors.

Il est interdit de fumer dans le bateau. La compagnie Brittany Ferries vous souhaite un bon voyage.

Answers:

1. Information desk/office
2. Opposite the restaurant
3. Forbidden during the crossing
4. Go outside
5. Smoke

2B TRAVEL AND TRANSPORT (2)

READING

Answers:

1. B
2. D
3. C
4. A
5. B
6. D
7. B
8. A

READING

Answers:

1. 5%
2. Tram, bus, bike
3. 19%
4. 6%
5. Yes
6. Tram, bus

WRITING

Suggested translations:

1. Il y a beaucoup d'embouteillages au centre-ville.
2. J'allais au collège à pied tous les jours.
3. Comment vas-tu au travail ?
4. J'aimerais avoir ma propre voiture.

READING

Suggested translations:

1. Everyone is on the road/travelling by road.
2. Some people are returning home.
3. For the majority of people it's going on holiday.
4. We already have some traffic jams.

GRAMMAR EXTRA

Answers:

- malheureusement
- vraiment
- mieux

LISTENING

Transcript:

Voici les infos routières pour aujourd'hui, le huit août.

Tout le monde est en route. Pour quelques-uns c'est le retour chez eux et pour la majorité c'est le départ en vacances. Alors attention sur les routes. Nous avons déjà des embouteillages à signaler.

La route A7 entre Lyon et Orange est complètement bloquée. Depuis ce matin, les autoroutes en direction des côtes et du sud ont des bouchons. Il faut compter trois heures de retard sur l'A7.

Sur l'A9 entre Perpignan et l'Espagne, les trajets prennent trois fois plus de temps que d'habitude.

La 61 est très chargée entre Toulouse et Narbonne.

Bison Futé conseille aux automobilistes d'éviter l'A49 avant Grenoble.

Entre Niort et Bordeaux, le trafic se ralentit dans les deux sens et il faut compter quatre heures de route.

Enfin, un accident ralentit encore les voitures au nord de Moulins avec douze bouchons.

Alors faites attention si vous partez en vacances ce weekend !

Answers:

Destinations	Lyon–Orange	Perpignan–Spain	Niort–Bordeaux	Moulins
Motorway (letter + number)	A7	A9		
Traffic problem	Road completely blocked since this morning on the motorway to the coast and the south	Journeys taking three times as long as usual	Slow moving traffic both ways	Accident slowing traffic down. Twelve bottle necks/traffic jams
Time of delay	Three hours		Four hours	

2B TRAVEL AND TRANSPORT (3)

READING

Answers:

1. voyageurs
2. septembre
3. bagage
4. pouvez
5. billets
6. aller
7. est
8. bureau

EXTRA

Extra – Suggested translations:

1. There are more than three million travellers per year.
2. In September more travellers leave for Montreal.
3. A luggage surplus costs €80.
4. With access to free Wi-Fi, you can surf the Internet as much as you like.

READING

Answers:

1. A little bit behind Lucien
2. Down the stairs
3. Have you got/does she have a ticket?
4. She doesn't have one
5. An old man
6. Read the names of the stations

LISTENING

Transcript.

Caissier : Bonjour Madame, je peux vous aider ?

Femme : Bonjour, je voudrais réserver des billets pour l'Allemagne s'il vous plaît.

Caissier : Pas de problème. C'est pour quelle date et à quelle heure ?

Femme : C'est pour le quinze mars vers quatorze heures si possible.

Caissier : D'accord. C'est pour combien de personnes ?

Femme : Quatre personnes.

Caissier : Et c'est pour des adultes ou des enfants ?

Femme : Une adulte et trois enfants.

Caissier : Voulez-vous des allers-retours ?

Femme : Oui, s'il vous plaît. Ça fait combien ?

Caissier : Voyons, ça fait cent cinquante euros s'il vous plaît. Comment voulez-vous payer ?

Femme : Je peux payer par carte de crédit ?

Caissier : Oui pas de problème. Alors voici vos billets et je vous souhaite un bon voyage. Au revoir.

Femme : Merci monsieur, au revoir.

Answers:

1. a
2. b
3. c
4. c
5. a

2A LOCAL AREAS OF INTEREST
2B TRAVEL AND TRANSPORT
GRAMMAR IN CONTEXT

GRAMMAR

1. IMPERFECT TENSE

1. J'écrivais un blog tous les jours.
2. J'allais en vacances tous les ans.
3. Il jouait au tennis tous les étés.
4. Il pleuvait tous les jours.

2. COMMANDS

1. Visite le musée !
2. Donnez-moi le portable !
3. Prenons la rue à gauche !
4. Regarde à droite !
5. Tournez à gauche !

3. CONDITIONAL

1. Nous **mangerions** au restaurant.
2. J'**achèterais** une maison.
3. Il **habiterait** en ville.
4. Ils **visiteraient** la campagne.
5. Mes parents **vendraient** leur maison.

4. ADJECTIVES: COMPARATIVES AND SUPERLATIVES

1. Une voiture est plus **chère** qu'un vélo.
   A car is more expensive than a bike.
2. Les avions sont les plus **impressionnants**.
   Planes are the most amazing.
3. Un livre est moins **intéressant** qu'une tablette.
   A book is less interesting than a tablet.
4. Un taxi est aussi **grand** qu'une voiture.
   A taxi is as big as a car.

5. ADVERBS

Accept any suitable answers

6. PRESENT TENSE

1. Je **vais** en voiture.
2. Il y **a** un restaurant.
3. Ma ville **est** ennuyeuse.
4. Le musée **ouvre** à 9 heures.
5. On **achète** un billet au guichet.

THEME: CURRENT AND FUTURE STUDY AND EMPLOYMENT

UNIT 1

CURRENT STUDY

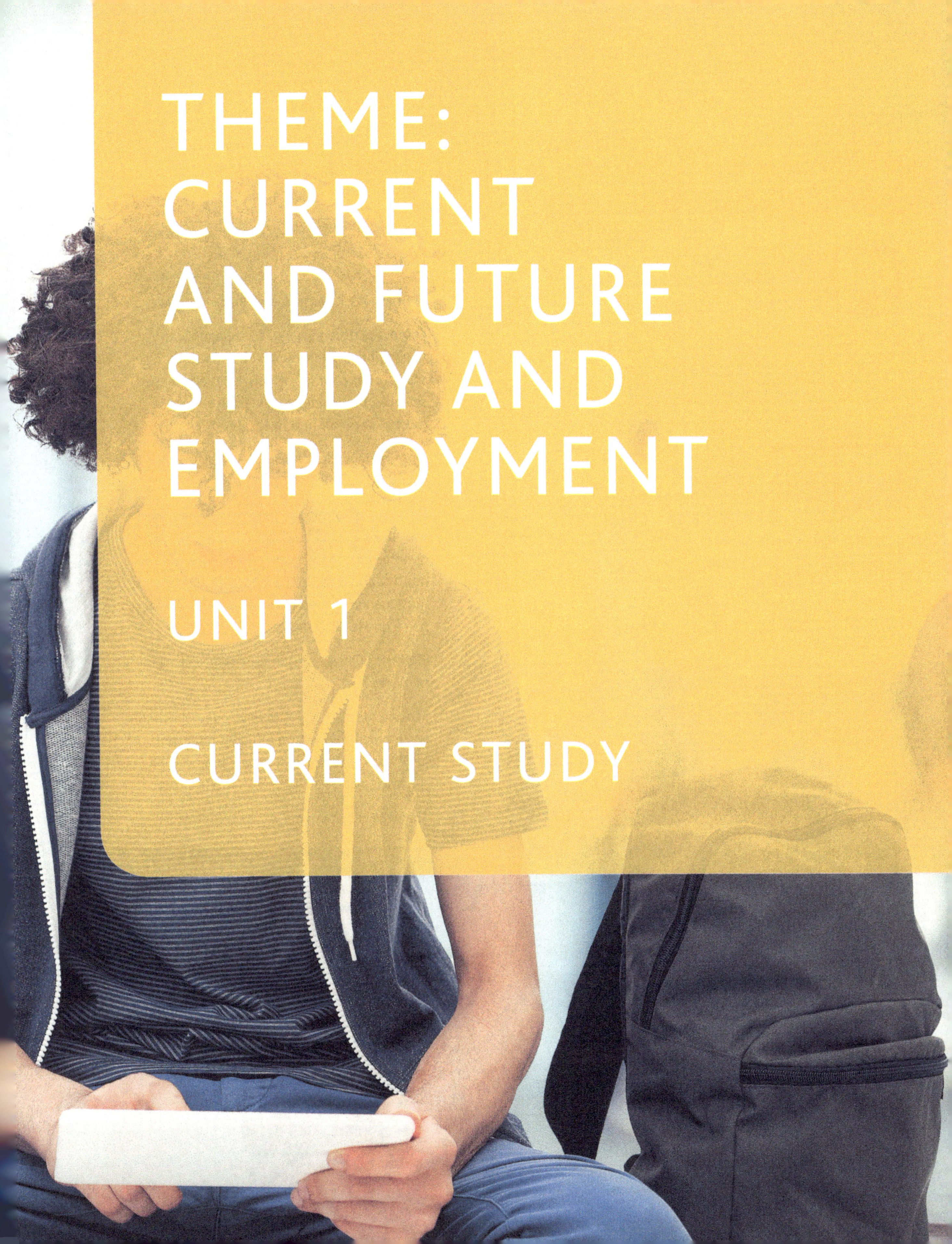

3A SCHOOL/ COLLEGE LIFE (1)

READING

Answers:

1. 25 heures 30
2. 9 heures
3. 2 heures
4. 4 heures 30
5. Français et maths
6. Éducation civique et sociale

READING

Answers:

1. Next to Delphine
2. The maths teacher
3. To avoid chatting
4. Make a noise
5. Name and class
6. Spanish
7. Clapped hands

LISTENING

Transcript:

Homme : Quelles matières étudies-tu à l'école ?

Femme : J'étudie l'anglais, l'espagnol, la géographie et la musique. Mes matières obligatoires sont le français, les maths et les sciences. Mes matières facultatives sont la musique et l'informatique.

Homme : Quelle matière préfères-tu ? Et pourquoi ?

Femme : Je préfère les langues parce qu'elles sont utiles quand on est à l'étranger. Je suis orientée vers les langues, mais j'aime aussi les maths parce que c'est une matière logique. La musique est intéressante et j'adore la biologie parce que je la trouve facile.

Homme : Qu'est-ce que tu n'aimes pas comme matières ?

Femme : Je n'aime pas la physique ni la chimie parce qu'elles sont trop difficiles pour moi. Je déteste les sports parce que je ne suis pas sportive.

The correct statements are 2, 3, 6, 8, 9, 10

3A SCHOOL/ COLLEGE LIFE (2)

READING

Answers:

1. e
2. a
3. f
4. i
5. d
6. c
7. j
8. g
9. h
10. b

READING

Answers:

1. B.F.
2. A.M.
3. S.P.
4. G.R.
5. H.K.

EXTRA

Extra – Suggested translations:

S.P.: I had 7/20 in French today! My friend who is originally from the United States had 12/20!

H.K: Before a test my teacher asked me which language it was today – English or German?

READING

Suggested translations:

1. I ate in the canteen and it was delicious.
2. I like school, but the teachers are strict.
3. You must always be on time.
4. My ideal school would be very big with lots of computers.

WRITING

EXTRA

Extra – Suggested translations:

Je suis très fatigué parce que j'ai trop de devoirs !
I am very tired because I have too much homework!

Ici on ne porte pas d'uniforme scolaire.
Here we don't wear school uniform.

D'habitude je porte un jean et un t-shirt.
Usually I wear jeans and a T-shirt.

LISTENING

Transcript:

Julie : Je m'appelle Julie, j'ai dix-sept ans. J'ai un niveau correct en anglais, mais mon accent est terrible ! Je regarde les films en version originale pour essayer d'améliorer ma prononciation, mais je n'y arrive pas ! Que conseilles-tu ?

Imagine que tu joues un rôle au théâtre. Utilise ton imagination et regarde ton visage dans un miroir. Concentre-toi sur l'intonation.

Louis : Je suis Louis et j'ai seize ans. Depuis la quatrième je suis nul en maths. Je trouve l'algèbre difficile. Je fais mes devoirs, je révise, mais quand il y a un contrôle, c'est la panique !

Le blocage arrive quand on est stressé. Calme-toi en respirant bien. Révise en ligne ou avec un ami au lieu d'être seul. Il existe de nombreux jeux sur Internet. Essaie-les et amuse-toi un peu avec les maths.

Answers:

Julie: She thinks she has a bad English accent. She is advised to imagine she is acting a part in the theatre, or to look at herself talking in a mirror and to concentrate on her intonation.

Louis: He finds maths hard, particularly algebra, and he panics when he has a test. He is advised to keep calm and breathe deeply. He is also advised to play maths games on the computer or revise with a friend and to enjoy himself when doing maths.

3A SCHOOL/ COLLEGE LIFE (3)

READING

Answers:

1. Outskirts of Lyon
2. 60
3. New and modern
4. Literature studies, economics, social studies, sciences
5. Management, business, health and social care

READING

Answers:

1. sortes
2. rigolos
3. des
4. commun
5. sont
6. aiment
7. qui
8. questions

LISTENING

Before undertaking the listening exercise, some preparatory work will need to be done on the differences between French and British schools.

Transcript:

1. On commence à neuf heures.
2. On commence la journée avec l'appel.
3. On commence à huit heures.
4. Il faut porter une jupe grise et une chemise blanche.
5. Nous avons une heure et demie pour la pause déjeuner.
6. Il faut acheter notre matériel scolaire.
7. Je rentre chez moi à dix-sept heures.
8. L'école nous donne des cahiers.

Answers:

1. Grande Bretagne
2. Grande Bretagne
3. France
4. Grande Bretagne
5. France
6. France
7. France
8. Grande Bretagne

WRITING

Answers:

1. Il est interdit de porter des bijoux.
2. C'est un vieux collège.
3. Le collège commence à neuf heures moins le quart.
4. Les sciences sont utiles.
5. Les langues sont importantes.

3B SCHOOL/ COLLEGE STUDIES (1)

READING

Answers:

1. B
2. C
3. E
4. F
5. A

EXTRA

Extra –Suggested translations:

1. I would like to be a vet, so I must study the sciences.
2. I would like to become a mechanic and I would like to work with cars.
3. Well, I would like to be a football coach. I am going to continue my sport studies at university.
4. I am interested in countries and nature. So, I would like to continue my studies in geography.
5. I would like to study Spanish because I love Spain and I would like to live there.

READING

Answers:

Course	Languages
Hours per week	Eight
Foreign languages	Spanish, Italian
Regional languages	Breton, Corsican, Basque
Other areas studied	Civilisation, way of life, different attitudes
Details of language course	New vocabulary, grammar, conversation, studying texts, documents, films and translation

Course	Sport
Hours per week	Nine
Other areas studied	Health, business, safety, events
Activities	Two physical/sport/artistic activities

LISTENING

Transcript:

Martin : Marianne, est-ce que les cours au lycée sont différents des cours au collège ?

Marianne : Ne t'inquiète pas trop mon petit. Tu continueras d'étudier le français, l'histoire-géo et les maths.

Martin : Quelles sont les nouvelles matières pour moi ?

Marianne : Alors, tu peux étudier l'économie, les sciences médicales, la physique-chimie où la littérature.

Martin : Comment sont les profs ?

Marianne : Les profs au lycée sont très exigeants. Ils parlent plus vite. Tu auras aussi plus de devoirs !

Answers:

1. Not to worry
2. French, history, geography, maths
3. Economics, medical sciences, physics, chemistry and literature
4. More demanding and talk fast
5. You will have more homework

3B SCHOOL/ COLLEGE STUDIES (2)

READING

Answers:

1. Maths
2. History, French, art
3. Based on historical periods/times
4. She had a vivid imagination
5. Poems
6. At home/in her house
7. Grandmother

READING

Answers:

Luc: Listens in class but doesn't understand.
Advice: Work on long-term memory, work with a friend, revise a little each day.

Stéphanie: Doesn't like talking in front of others in class. She is shy when it comes to speaking.
Advice: Breathe, relax. Practise in front of a mirror in her bedroom and then in front of friends/family.

Fiona: Finds it hard to concentrate in class and is always tired.
Advice: Go to bed one hour earlier each day and switch off phone/iPod or leave in the lounge.

READING

Suggested translations:

1. I like history but I find it difficult.
2. I did lots of homework yesterday – especially maths.
3. My sister doesn't listen in class.
4. I would like to study German because I would like to work in Germany.

LISTENING

Transcript:

Anne : Nous avons deux types de classes – monolingue (ça veut dire tous les cours sont en français) et bilingue (la moitié des cours en français et l'autre moitié en breton). Ce sont les familles qui font le choix.

Aujourd'hui par exemple, les enfants ont les maths et le français le matin en langue française. Et l'après-midi l'histoire-géo qu'on enseigne en breton.

On fait aussi la gymnastique en breton et en français. Cette année nous avons cinquante élèves qui suivent les cours en classes bilingues et trente-huit élèves qui prennent les cours seulement en français.

Answers:

1. a	3. c	5. b	7. c
2. b	4. c	6. c	

WRITING

Suggested translations:

1. En ce moment j'ai beaucoup de devoirs à faire.
2. Je suis vraiment content d'avoir choisi d'étudier l'EPS et le français.
3. Ma sœur adore lire et elle est forte en anglais.
4. Je trouve les maths difficiles, mais mon prof m'aide beaucoup.
5. Je ne suis pas créatif et j'ai de mauvaises notes en dessin.

3B SCHOOL/ COLLEGE STUDIES (3)

READING

Answers:

1. Une fille de ma classe m'embête
2. On a trop de contrôles
3. On doit redoubler l'année
4. Il y a une retenue
5. Un nouveau collège
6. Je dois travailler
7. Ils nous donnent
8. Tout est stressant
9. Je n'ai pas envie d'
10. Je me sens seul(e)

EXTRA

Extra - suggested translations:

1. If we don't make enough progress we have to retake the year.
2. They give us some lines to write.
3. If we don't do the homework, there is a detention.
4. My parents make me stressed and the teachers make me stressed – everything is stressful!
5. We have too many tests and homework.
6. I have to work for at least three hours every night doing homework – it's too much!
7. I haven't got any friends in class, so I feel all alone!
8. A girl in my class annoys me, there are some days where I don't feel like going to school because of her!
9. Last year my father changed his place of work and I had to enrol in a new school.

READING

Answers:

1. préparation	5. aurais	9. semaines
2. pas	6. ai	10. bien
3. vraiment	7. avance	11. trop
4. éviter	8. naturel	12. dormir

LISTENING

Transcript:

Pour être bien préparé pour un contrôle ou un examen, il faut bien dormir la nuit. La recommandation est de dormir au moins huit heures. S'il faut se lever à six heures et demie, il faut se coucher vers vingt-deux heures.

Pour se réveiller, demande à tes parents de te faire lever avec une voix douce. Sinon tu peux utiliser un réveil qui simule la lumière du jour.

Le matin d'un examen, prends une douche chaude. Pour le petit déjeuner, bois un jus d'orange et mange des céréales avec du lait ou une tartine avec de la confiture. Évite les produits sucrés.

Answers:

1. Parents, doucement (voix)
2. Prends une douche chaude
3. Jus d'orange, des céréales avec du lait ou une tartine avec de la confiture
4. Produits sucrés

3A SCHOOL/COLLEGE LIFE
3B SCHOOL/COLLEGE STUDIES
GRAMMAR IN CONTEXT

GRAMMAR

1. THE PERFECT TENSE WITH *AVOIR*

Suggested translations:

1. J'ai **fait** mes devoirs.
2. J'ai **mangé** un sandwich dans la cantine.
3. Il a **étudié** dans la bibliothèque.
4. Les professeurs ont **donné** beaucoup de travail.
5. Nous avons **travaillé** très dur.

2. THE PERFECT TENSE WITH *ÊTRE*

1. Elle est **rentrée** à la maison.
2. Nous sommes **arrivé(e)s** au collège à neuf heures.
3. Ils sont **entrés** dans la salle de classe.
4. Comment es-tu **allé(e)** au collège ?
5. Je suis **retourné(e)** à mon école primaire.
6. Ma sœur s'est **couchée** tard parce qu'elle avait beaucoup de devoirs.

3. *ÊTRE* OR *AVOIR*?

1. Elle **est** revenue à notre classe.
2. Nous **avons** pris l'autobus ce matin.
3. **Avez**-vous entendu l'explication du professeur ?
4. Mes amis **sont** arrivés pendant la récré.
5. Les profs **sont** restés dans la salle des professeurs.
6. Il **a** décidé d'étudier les sciences.

4. THE TIME

1. Les cours commencent à huit heures et demie.
2. La recrée commence à onze heures vingt.
3. L'école finit à quatre heures moins vingt-cinq.
4. Je me couche à dix heures et quart.
5. Je me lève à sept heures moins le quart.

5. INDEFINITE ADJECTIVES

Suggested translations:

1. Some pupils forgot their homework.
2. My brother hates all the subjects.
3. The other pupils study biology.
4. Each pupil has to wear a tie.
5. My teacher says the same thing every day.
6. There are several strict teachers in my school.

6. OBJECT PRONOUNS

1. Il l'aime.
2. Je l'ai fait.
3. J'y vais.
4. J'en ai beaucoup.
5. Le professeur le lui donne.

THEME: IDENTITY AND CULTURE

UNIT 2

LIFESTYLE

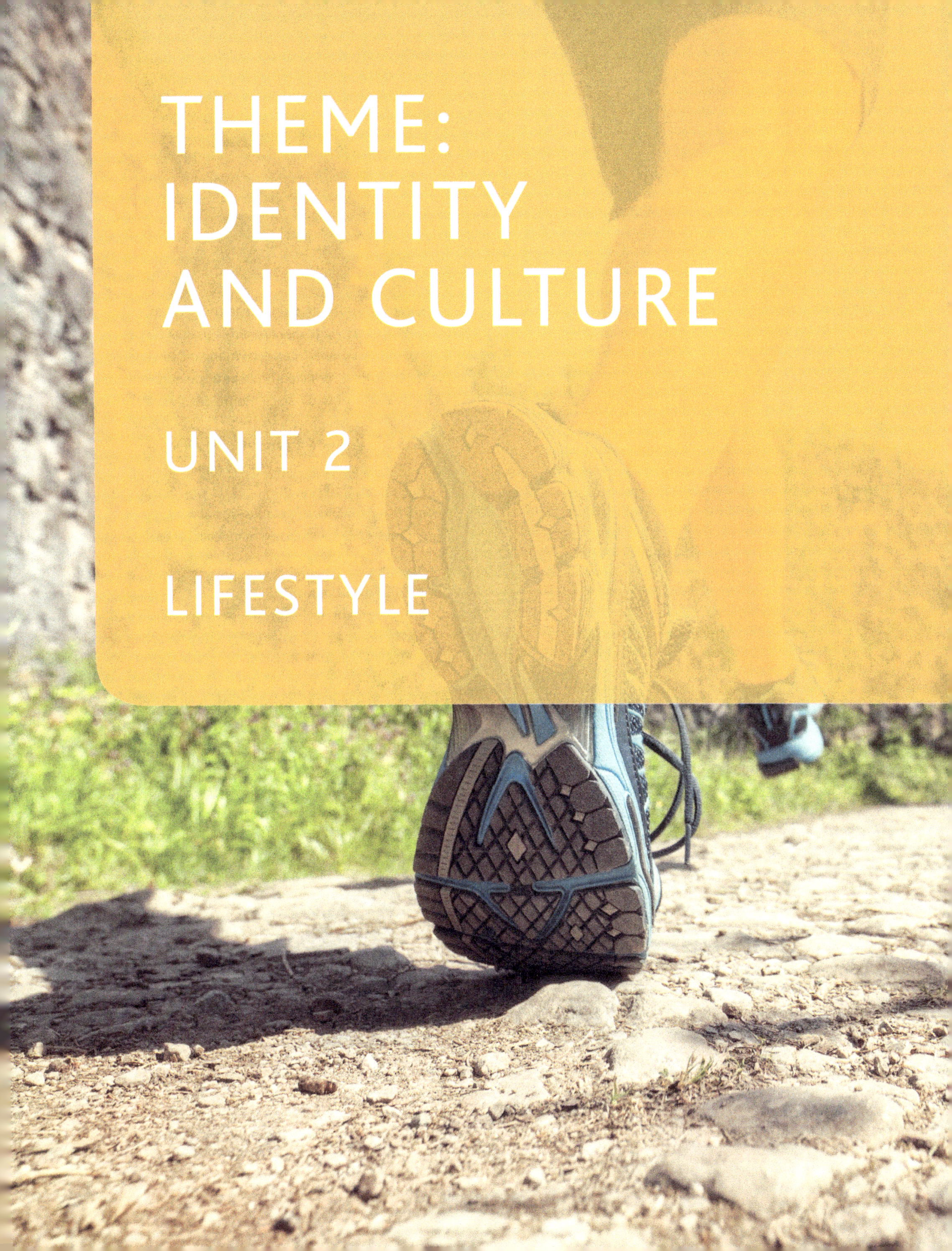

4A HEALTH AND FITNESS (1)

READING

Answers:

1. Guy
2. Eliane
3. Guy
4. Julie
5. Guy
6. Baptiste

EXTRA

Extra

- J'ai toujours faim
- J'essaie de manger sain
- Je suis en forme
- Grignoter
- Je sais qu'il faut faire plus

READING

Answers:

The correct statements are 1, 4, 6, 7, 8

LISTENING

Transcript:

En France, manger, boire ou grignoter prennent deux heures vingt-deux minutes par personne par jour. La plupart des gens mangent toujours les trois repas principaux : le petit déjeuner, le déjeuner et le dîner. La moitié des français mangent le déjeuner vers treize heures. Quinze pourcent grignotent pendant la journée.

Vingt pourcent des Français mangent devant la télé et ce sont les jeunes âgés de vingt-quatre ans qui le font le plus. Quelques-uns aiment lire ou écouter de la musique en mangeant.

Answers:

1. 2 hours 22 minutes
2. Three main meals: breakfast, lunch, dinner
3. Half
4. 20%
5. 24 years
6. Read or listen to music

4A HEALTH AND FITNESS (2)

READING

Answers:

1. a	4. c	7. d
2. d	5. a	
3. a	6. d	

READING

Answers:

1. entre	4. entraîné	7. dors
2. répondu	5. vie	8. beaucoup
3. dernière	6. garder	

WRITING

Suggested translation:

J'adore la voile et je suis membre de l'équipe Olympique de France. Je suis en bonne santé et je mange beaucoup de fruits et de légumes. Je ne mange jamais de fast food. Je ne bois pas d'alcool et je ne fume pas. Je me couche de bonne heure. Cette année, je voudrais gagner la médaille d'or aux Jeux Olympiques. Alors, il est vraiment important de garder la forme.

LISTENING

Transcript:

Cet été, viens jouer au tennis au club de tennis à Quiberon. Tu peux nous trouver en face de l'école de voile au bord de la mer. Nous sommes ouverts de neuf heures à midi et quart le matin et de seize heures à vingt heures le soir.

Il y a quatre courts dehors et un couvert. Nous avons aussi un mur d'entraînement dehors. Dans le club house il y a un bar, des vestiaires et des douches.

Au mois de juillet, les jeunes peuvent s'inscrire aux tournois. Au mois d'août, les adultes peuvent s'inscrire aux tournois.

Comme tarif, on peut louer les courts de tennis par heure. Les courts dehors coûtent treize euros et le court à l'intérieur coûte quinze euros.

Pour nous contacter: téléphone au zéro deux, quatre-vingt-sept, soixante, quarante-trois.

Answers:

1. Tennis club
2. Opposite the sailing school near the sea
3. 9.00–12.15 and 16.00–20.00
4. Four outside courts, one inside court, training wall, bar, changing rooms, showers
5. Tournaments for young people
6. €13 for outside court, €15 for inside court
7. 02 87 60 43

4A HEALTH AND FITNESS (3)

READING

Answers:

1. Down
2. 7
3. More
4. Young people
5. 17
6. Three glasses

READING

Answers:

The false sentences are 2, 4, 7, 8

EXTRA

Extra:

1. Young people drink a lot of alcohol.
3. You can die if you drink too much alcohol and smoke cannabis.
5. Adults drink less than young people.
6. 50% of young people have done binge drinking (or drunk to excess).

LISTENING

Transcript:

Selon une enquête, les Français deviennent plus gros. Trente-neuf pourcent des hommes et vingt-quatre pourcent des femmes ont des kilos en trop. Il y a des facteurs génétiques bien sûr, mais la raison principale est qu'ils mangent trop et font moins d'exercices. Les Français grignotent plus et utilisent la technologie au lieu de faire de l'exercice.

Il est important que les gens obèses perdent du poids en mangeant plus sainement. Il faut éviter le sucre et les matières grasses qui sont souvent cachés dans les produits alimentaires. Fais attention aux yaourts et à la confiture sucrés. Avant d'aller au supermarché, fais une liste et évite les rayons biscuits et gâteaux. En plus, il faut éviter les boissons gazeuses telles que le cola. Un verre de cola contient six cuillères de sucre. Trop de sucre augmente le risque de diabète.

Answers:

1. Les Français deviennent gros
2. 24%
3. Manger trop et ne pas faire assez d'exercices
4. Les produits sucrés/gras
5. Avoir une liste, éviter les rayons biscuits et gâteaux
6. Six

READING

Suggested translation:

Aquagym is a good exercise to keep in shape. You exercise in the water. It's a good sport to do in the morning. Aquagym is good for your mind and body. Everyone can do it in a swimming pool near to one's home.

4B ENTERTAINMENT AND LEISURE (1)

READING

Answers:

1. Jerôme
2. Lila
3. Émilie
4. Pierre, Lila, Jerôme
5. Émilie
6. Pierre, Jerôme
7. Pierre
8. Émilie
9. Lila, Pierre
10. Jerôme

READING

Answers:

Plot: Set in the 1920s, an era of jazz and illegal alcohol smuggling. About a writer, Nick Carraway, who leaves the Midwest of America and goes to New York. He meets a mysterious millionaire called Jay Gatsby who has lots of big parties. Fascinated by the millionaires he meets, Nick writes a story about love, dreams and tragedies.

Characters:
Nick, a writer, wants to be part of the American dream.
Jay, a millionaire who has big parties and loves socialising.

Review/opinion: Captivating and romantic. The story mirrors modern society.

LISTENING

Transcript:

Interviewer : Les jeunes deviennent de plus en plus branchés aux jeux vidéo. Lucas, dis-moi ce que tu fais.

Lucas : Je joue souvent aux jeux sur l'ordinateur et maintenant j'ai des problèmes au collège parce que mes notes ont vraiment baissé.

Interviewer : Si on joue trop, on n'a pas assez de temps pour le reste tel que les études, dormir, être en famille, faire du sport par exemple. Le problème principal c'est que tu ne te disciplines pas. Tes parents peuvent t'aider.

Lucas : Qu'est-ce qu'ils peuvent faire ?

Interviewer : Il est important qu'ils établissent un temps pour jouer qui est raisonnable. On peut mettre une limite au temps avec l'ordinateur et après avoir utilisé ce temps, l'ordinateur s'arrête.

Answers:

1. ordinateur
2. ses notes sont mauvaises/se baissent
3. ses études, dormir, être avec sa famille
4. parents
5. mettre une limite au temps avec l'ordinateur

4B ENTERTAINMENT AND LEISURE (2)

READING

Answers:

1. d	3. d	5. b	7. c
2. a	4. b	6. d	8. c

READING

Answers:

	Restaurant Gaudi	La Strada
Location	Opposite train station	Town centre
Nationality	Spanish	Italian
Dish of the day	Potato omelette	Salmon pizza
Drinks	Included	Free glass of wine for adults, free glass of juice for children before 8pm
Service included?	No	Yes
Day closed	Tuesday	Monday
Cost of menu of the day	€25	€30

READING

Suggested translation:

It's difficult when I go out and eat in a restaurant with my friends. I am vegetarian and I am allergic to fish! I don't like fizzy drinks. When I choose a meal in a restaurant I always have to ask about the ingredients. Fortunately, I love chocolate and fruit, so desserts aren't a problem for me!

WRITING

Suggested translations:

1. Je dépense plus d'argent quand je sors avec mon ami(e).
2. La semaine prochaine j'irai au cinéma avec ma sœur.
3. Quel est ton passe-temps préféré ?
4. Je suis allergique au fromage.
5. Je ne peux pas sortir ce soir parce que j'ai trop de devoirs.

LISTENING

Transcript:

Bonsoir, ici Claire. Je veux laisser un message pour Angie. Le film commence à vingt et une heures et demie. Alors, si on se retrouvait au café du cinéma vers vingt et une heures ? Mon père peut venir nous chercher après le film. Sylvie ne vient pas parce qu'elle n'a pas assez d'argent. Charlotte ne vient pas non plus car elle fait du babysitting pour sa sœur. Alors à toute à l'heure.

Answers:

1. Message
2. 21.30
3. Café
4. Dad
5. Not enough money
6. Babysitting

4B ENTERTAINMENT AND LEISURE (3)

READING

Answers:

1. Play
2. Hide and seek, seven families, little horses
3. She doesn't want to play
4. Tidy her bedroom
5. A week

READING

Answers:

The correct statements are 2, 4, 6, 9, 10

EXTRA

Extra – Suggested translations:

2. We think that we haven't got enough free time.
4. The French have 4 hours 58 minutes leisure time.
6. Sandrine cuts hair at work.
9. Every day is the same.
10. In the evening she puts her children to bed.

LISTENING

Transcript:

Le nouveau groupe de musique, qui s'appelle TIC TAC, est très jeune. L'âge moyen est douze ans. Ils se voient chaque mercredi soir pour jouer. Cette année ils ont six concerts en Bretagne. Le premier concert sera le huit juin à Carnac. Le groupe se compose de trois garçons et deux filles. Ils préparent leur premier disque et ils écrivent leurs propres chansons. La semaine prochaine ils vont enregistrer leur disque dans un studio. Pour en savoir plus, consultez leur site web, www.tictacmusique.fr.

Answers:

1. A new music group
2. 12 years old
3. Every Wednesday evening
4. Playing concerts
5. Three
6. Recording their new record

4A HEALTH AND FITNESS
4B ENTERTAINMENT AND LEISURE
GRAMMAR IN CONTEXT

GRAMMAR

1. DEMONSTRATIVE ADJECTIVES

1. Ce sport
2. Ces filles
3. Cette personne
4. Ces hommes

2. PRESENT TENSE REFLEXIVE VERBS

1. Vous <u>vous couchez</u>
2. Nous <u>nous levons</u>
3. Je <u>m'habille</u>
4. Ils <u>se lavent</u>

3. RELATIVE PRONOUNS

1. qui
2. que
3. que
4. qu'
5. que

4. CONJUNCTIONS

Accept any suitable answer.

5. THE PRESENT PARTICIPLE

Suggested answers:

1. Elle est rentrée en pleurant.
2. Ils ont bavardé en regardant la télé.
3. En criant, elle a appelé son père.
4. Il a vu ses amis en finissant le jeu.

6. TENSES WITH *SI*

Suggested translations:

1. If I could have spoken to him, I would have gone with him.
2. If I were to come, I could help you.

THEME: WALES AND THE WORLD – AREAS OF INTEREST

UNIT 2

THE WIDER WORLD

5A LOCAL AND REGIONAL FEATURES AND CHARACTERISTICS OF FRANCE AND FRENCH-SPEAKING COUNTRIES (1)

READING

Answers:

1. Sud-ouest de l'océan Indien
2. Trois
3. Beaux paysages, plages
4. Canne à sucre, thé
5. 25°C
6. Fortes pluies, entre 25 à 30°C, des orages

READING

Answers:

The correct statements are 2, 3, 6, 7, 10

EXTRA

Extra:

1. se trouve
2. environ
3. beaucoup à voir
4. attire
5. accueille
6. le monde
7. contre

LISTENING

Transcript:

Voici nos idées pour les sorties de weekend dans les alentours d'Auray.

Spectacle pour les enfants samedi après-midi à Quiberon. Venez voir notre magicien et amusez-vous avec des sketchs pour les petits. À dix-huit heures aux jardins Brétino. Entrée gratuite.

Samedi soir au port de Locmariaquer à vingt et une heures, soirée d'été pour toute la famille avec danses bretonnes et barbecue. Prix cinq euros.

Pour une balade nocturne pour adultes, venez à Saint-Anne-d'Auray samedi soir à vingt heures. Apportez une torche ou utilisez votre portable pour avoir de la lumière. Réservation obligatoire peut se faire à l'office de tourisme. Balade gratuite.

Dimanche après-midi à quatorze heures, visite à la ferme de la baie à Erdeven. Essayez les produits puis rapportez-en chez vous ! Tarif : deux euros pour adultes, gratuit pour les moins de douze ans.

Answers:

	Quiberon	Locmariaquer	Saint-Anne-d'Auray	Erdeven
Type of outing	Show, sketches, magician	Summer evening with Breton dancing, BBQ	Night walk	Farm visit
When?	Saturday 6pm	Saturday 9pm	Saturday 8pm	Sunday 2pm
Cost?	Free	€5	Free	€2 adults, children free
Who for?	Children	Families	Adults	Adults and children

5A LOCAL AND REGIONAL FEATURES AND CHARACTERISTICS OF FRANCE AND FRENCH-SPEAKING COUNTRIES (2)

READING

Answers:

1. Futuroscope
2. Disneyland Paris
3. Château et musée des ducs de Bretagne
4. Château et musée des ducs de Bretagne
5. L'Abbaye de Mont-Saint-Michel
6. Disneyland Paris
7. Futuroscope
8. L'Abbaye de Mont-Saint-Michel

READING

Answers:

1. Found at end of Rue Montueuse, near castle
2. Not busy, hot in summer, cold in winter (any two)
3. Clean and dry
4. Found in the old part of the town
5. Solid, made from wood
6. Admired them

LISTENING

Transcript:

On recommande un mini-séjour à Strasbourg, la capitale de l'Alsace. Un des meilleurs endroits pour passer un weekend en couple ou avec des amis. Strasbourg est une ville historique avec un marché célèbre à Noël. Il faut visiter la cathédrale gothique.

La ville offre de nombreux restaurants, cafés et bars et le centre-ville est très animé le soir. Si la culture vous intéresse, visitez un ou deux musées: le musée Alsacien et le musée archéologique sont incontournables.

N'oubliez pas de faire un tour en bateau-promenade, et aussi de visiter le jardin des deux Rives. L'Allemagne est à quelques pas de là.

Answers:

1. c	3. a	5. b	7. c
2. b	4. a	6. b	8. c

READING

Suggested translation:

Disneyland Paris has some interesting statistics.

1. Tourists eat more than four million hamburgers each year.
2. The oldest tourist was 106 years old.
3. There are over 150 chefs.
4. You can eat in more than 68 different restaurants.
5. 500,000 flowers are planted each year.

5A LOCAL AND REGIONAL FEATURES AND CHARACTERISTICS OF FRANCE AND FRENCH-SPEAKING COUNTRIES (3)

READING

Answers:

1. North-west
2. Between the sea and mountains
3. Hot and dry
4. Small, modern and old
5. Medieval castle, two churches, cathedral
6. Train, plane, boat
7. 1436

LISTENING

Transcript:

Venez visiter le Stade de France où se passent tous les importants matchs de football et concerts à Paris.

Notre visite officielle dure une heure et on peut le réserver à l'avance. Les départs sont à onze heures, midi, quatorze heures et seize heures. Les visites sont en français et en anglais. Il y a aussi le musée à visiter.

Nous sommes fermés le lundi.

En raison de rénovations, les visites du Stade de France seront temporairement fermées entre le treize mai et le dix-sept juillet. Cependant, le musée sera toujours ouvert.

Answers:

1. Football matches, concerts
2. One hour
3. 4pm
4. English and French
5. Monday
6. Temporary closure due to renovation
7. No

READING

Answers:

The correct statements are 3, 4, 7, 8, 9

EXTRA

Extra:

3. Henry IV lived there.
4. There are about 10 rooms to see.
7. There will be a Middle Ages Show on a weekend in July.
8. On 4 August you can dance all night.
9. You have to choose your dinner in advance of the ball.

WRITING

Suggested translation:

Le château, construit en 1325, est une destination touristique très populaire. Il est ouvert tous les jours sauf le mardi. Je suis allé(e) au musée hier et il était vraiment intéressant. Demain je ferai du shopping.

5B HOLIDAYS AND TOURISM (1)

LISTENING

Transcript:

Section 1

Comment se sont passées tes vacances Simon ?

Simon : Cet été nous sommes allés dans les Pyrénées pour rendre visite à mes grands-parents. J'adore leur rendre visite parce que ma grand-mère fait mon gâteau préféré et je peux jouer avec les chiens et les promener dans les montagnes. Il a fait chaud, mais j'aime bien la chaleur.

Section 2

Et toi Alexandre comment étaient tes vacances ?

Alexandre : Moi, j'ai eu les pires vacances de ma vie. Nous sommes allés à Barcelone en Espagne, une ville qui me plaît énormément, mais toute la famille y était malade ! Alors nous avons dû rester au lit pendant deux jours et le dernier jour avant de rentrer il a plu à verse toute la journée. C'était un désastre !

Answers:

1. Summer
2. Grandparents
3. Played with dogs, walked in mountains
4. Hot
5. Worst holiday he has had/disaster because family was ill
6. He likes it a lot
7. Rained

READING

Answers:

1. D
2. B
3. A
4. C
5. B
6. C

READING

Answers:

	Review 1	Review 2	Review 3	Review 4
Date of review	12 January	20 May	3 January	November
Opinion	Exceptional service, quiet hotel	A good week Welcoming staff	High quality, exceptional service	Bad night's sleep because of noise from some customers
Information	Big luxury bedrooms, good location	Impeccable room and smart atmosphere	Must try the salmon and chocolate mousse in the restaurant	Breakfast served from 6am in quiet area

5B HOLIDAYS AND TOURISM (2)

READING

Answers:

1. Emma, Carl
2. Nathan, Laetitia, Carl
3. Véronique
4. Mathieu
5. Laetitia
6. Nathan
7. Emma

LISTENING

Transcript:

Le prix du jour à gagner ce sont des vacances pour deux personnes pour une semaine en Suisse. Vous séjournerez dans un hôtel de luxe et une bouteille de Champagne vous attend dans votre chambre.

Les repas au restaurant ne sont pas gratuits, mais le petit déjeuner est inclus. On vous offre deux billets d'avion en première classe.

Pour s'inscrire au concours il faut écrire cinquante mots au sujet de la Suisse. On ne peut recevoir qu'une participation par personne. La fin de jeu concours est le trente mai. Bonne chance et n'oubliez pas de donner votre nom, adresse et mail !

Answers:

Prize: holiday in Switzerland for two people for one week

Details of prize: luxury hotel, free bottle of champagne

Meals: meals not free, breakfast included

Travel: two first class plane tickets

How to enter: write 50 words about Switzerland, give your name, address, e-mail

Closing date: 30 May 2016

READING

Answers:

1. c
2. a
3. c
4. c
5. b

READING

Suggested translation:

Last year I went on holiday with my friends. We stayed with my penfriend, Annaëlle, who lives in Toulouse. We visited her in May. It was very hot. We liked the town a lot. Her family were very nice and I would like to go back there one day.

5B HOLIDAYS AND TOURISM (3)

READING

Answers:

1. 1.5% increase in visitors
2. July
3. Fine
4. Campsites, hotels
5. Holiday season
6. Economy
7. Problems parking, traffic jams

READING

Answers:

1. Afternoon
2. Black/dark
3. 600 km
4. Violent storm
5. Round, heavy, slow, stable

WRITING

Suggested translations:

1. La plupart des touristes restent dans les campings en vacances.
2. Quelques touristes se comportent mal en vacances.
3. La majorité des touristes prennent leurs vacances principales en été.
4. L'année dernière je suis allé(e) en vacances de sport avec mes amis.
5. À l'avenir j'aimerais aller en Australie.

LISTENING

Transcript:

Les colos de vacances accueillent des enfants âgés de six à douze ans. La colo à Monfort-sur-mer reçoit soixante-dix enfants par semaine.

Il y a beaucoup d'activités : on peut faire la cuisine, fabriquer des cerfs-volants, faire un montage vidéo, jouer dans des spectacles et plein de sports sont disponibles. Vendredi soir c'est toujours la fête !

Les enfants qui séjournent dans les colos habitent dans un rayon de cinquante kilomètres et leurs parents les y emmènent en voiture.

Les tarifs sont de cinquante-cinq euros par jour par enfant. Les sites les plus populaires se trouvent en Bretagne, Normandie, Auvergne et dans les Pays de la Loire.

Answers:

1. 6–12 ans
2. 70
3. Cuisine, fabriquer les cerfs-volants, faire un montage vidéo, spectacles et sports
4. Vendredi
5. Parents
6. 55 €
7. Bretagne/Normandie/L'Auvergne/Loire

5A LOCAL AND REGIONAL FEATURES AND CHARACTERISTICS OF FRANCE AND FRENCH-SPEAKING COUNTRIES

5B HOLIDAYS AND TOURISM

GRAMMAR IN CONTEXT

GRAMMAR

1. WEATHER VERBS

Suggested answers:

Lyon : Il y a du soleil.
Marseille : Il a été nuageux.
Nantes : Il pleuvait.
Strasbourg : Il neigera.
Bordeaux : Il ferait froid.

2. VERBS FOLLOWED BY PREPOSITIONS

Accept any suitable answers.

3. THE SUBJUNCTIVE

1. You must work.
2. I want you to stay.
3. I want to talk to you before you go out.
4. I am sorry that you are ill.

4. TALKING ABOUT A HOLIDAY IN THE PAST, PRESENT AND FUTURE

1. L'année dernière, je <u>**suis allé(e)**</u> en Espagne.
2. Il <u>**faisait**</u> beau tous les jours et le soleil <u>**brillait**</u>.
3. Nous <u>**avons passé**</u> deux nuits dans un hôtel au bord de la mer.
4. Normalement, je <u>**fais**</u> beaucoup d'activités aquatiques.
5. L'été prochain nous <u>**voyagerons**</u> en avion.

5. USING DIFFERENT TENSES TO TALK ABOUT HOLIDAYS

Accept any suitable answers in the same tense as the question:

1. Present
2. Imperfect
3. Perfect
4. Future
5. Conditional

6. PLUPERFECT TENSE

1. J'avais fini.
2. Il avait dit.
3. J'étais sorti.
4. Elle s'était couchée tard.

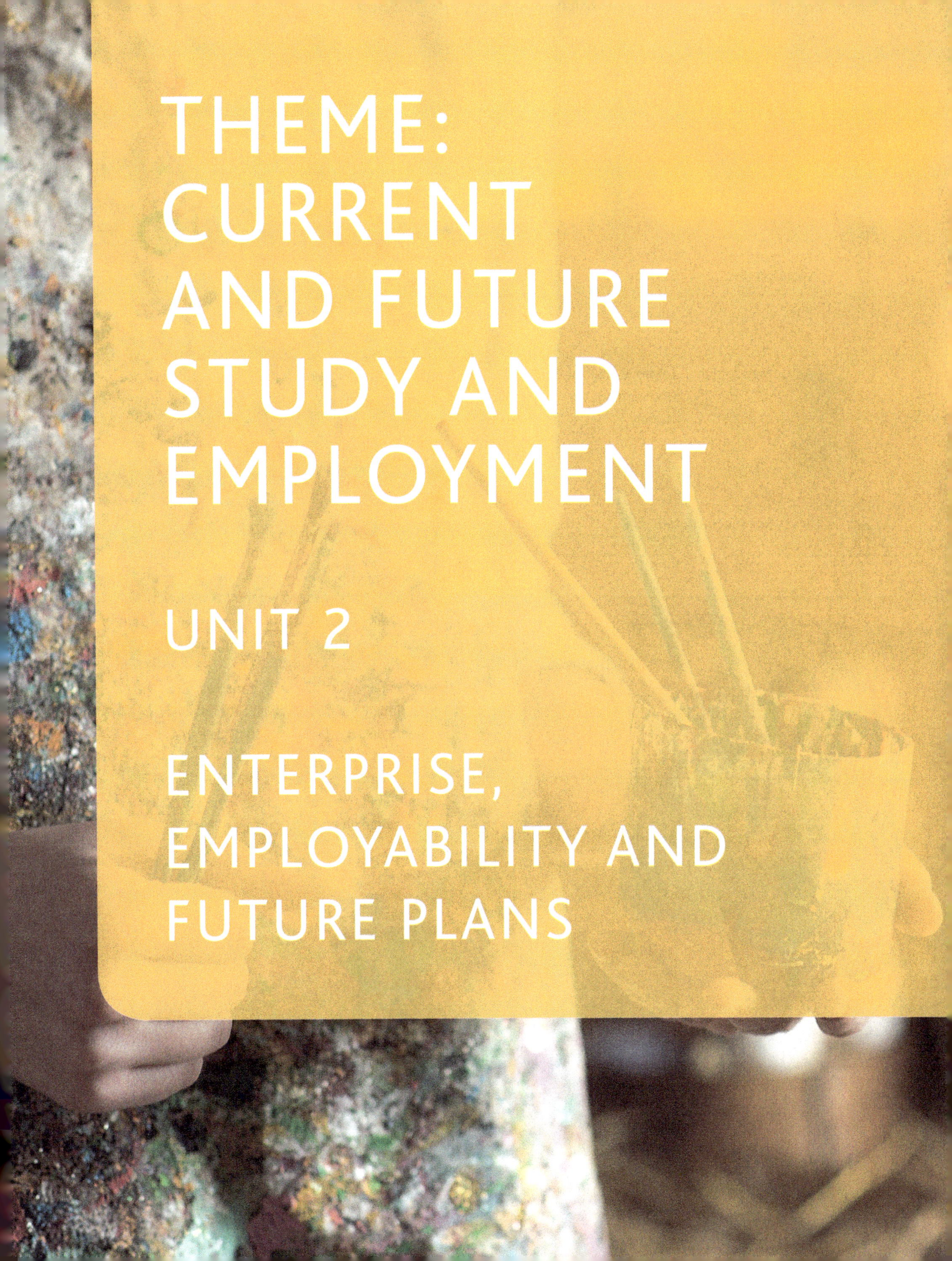

THEME: CURRENT AND FUTURE STUDY AND EMPLOYMENT

UNIT 2

ENTERPRISE, EMPLOYABILITY AND FUTURE PLANS

6A EMPLOYMENT (1)

READING

Answers:

	Mylène	Sébastien	Mari	Alain
Location	London	USA	Home	Holiday club
Job	Au pair	Woofing/odd jobs	Looking after pets/ pet sitting	Instructor for sports and sailing
Advantages of job	Improve English and earn pocket money	Stay with family for free	Like walking dogs	Gains experience and earns money

READING

Answers:

The correct statements are 3, 4, 7, 8, 10

LISTENING

Transcript:

Selon un sondage français sur les jeunes et l'argent, la plupart des jeunes sont conscients que l'argent ne tombe pas du ciel ! Les jeunes attribuent une forte valeur au travail. Quatre-vingt-dix pourcent des quinze à vingt ans disent qu'ils travaillent déjà ou veulent chercher un emploi.

Un jeune sur trois a un petit boulot déjà à partir de l'âge de quinze ans et plus. Quatre-vingts déclarent qu'ils mettent de l'argent de côté.

La majorité des jeunes dépensent leur argent pour un PC portable, un téléphone portable ou une soirée en boîte de nuit.

The correct statements are 2, 3, 6, 7, 9

6A EMPLOYMENT (2)

READING

Answers:

1. Office
2. Kind
3. If he was tired
4. Wash his hands
5. 12.30
6. Sea/port

READING

Answers:

Anne: Household jobs: washing dishes, vacuuming, washes car. Doesn't like it because it is tiring.

Luc: Works in supermarket. Doesn't like it because it is boring.

Marie: Looks after children after school and does babysitting at the weekend. Likes it.

Benjy: Coaches youngsters in football. Likes work.

Marc: Does nothing. Parents give him money and he hopes to get a summer job this year.

LISTENING

This is a gap fill exercise – the words are not provided in the textbook. You may prefer to give the words to the students in advance.

Transcript:

Pendant les grandes vacances, j'ai travaillé à la réception de l'hôtel près de chez moi. J'ai passé soixante-dix pourcent de mon temps à la réception. J'ai accueilli les clients à leur arrivée et lors de leur départ. J'ai fait des réservations pour le restaurant et j'ai pris des coups de téléphone. Quelquefois, j'ai travaillé de sept heures du matin au quatorze heures de l'après-midi et parfois, j'ai travaillé de quatorze heures à vingt et une heures. J'ai beaucoup aimé ce travail parce que je voudrais travailler plus tard dans la vie dans le tourisme. J'aime bien travailler en équipe et je me suis bien entendue avec mes collègues et les clients.

Answers:

1. grandes
2. près
3. passé
4. fait
5. pris
6. quelquefois
7. heures
8. parfois
9. voudrais
10. tard
11. travailler
12. entendue

WRITING

Suggested translation:

J'ai un petit boulot dans une boulangerie près de chez moi. Hier, j'ai commencé à sept heures du matin. Je devais me lever très tôt. Je travaille le samedi et l'après-midi je sors avec mes copains. J'aime mon boulot.

6A EMPLOYMENT (3)

READING

Answers:

David : Pharmacien
Sandrine : Instituteur
Baptiste : Coiffeur
Amandine : Facteur
Chloé : Hôtesse de l'air
Zac : Fermier

READING

Answers:

1. 26%
2. How much time to give
3. Association that helps families affected by cancer
4. Being in a football team
5. Six months
6. Wanted to do something useful and to help others
7. Developed confidence and gave her experience in the world of work
8. Do some voluntary work even if it is for a short time

LISTENING

Transcript:

J'ai commencé mon petit boulot d'été de disc-jockey parce que j'aime la musique et la technologie. J'ai eu de plus en plus de demandes et alors de plus en plus de travail ! J'ai dû m'organiser. J'ai été obligé de refuser quelques fêtes parce que j'ai trouvé que la voiture coûtait cher avec tous les trajets. Je dois rester au courant des dernières chansons et je dois adapter la musique selon la soirée.

Answers:

1. Liked music and technology
2. Has a lot of work
3. Organisational skills
4. Costs a lot to go by car
5. Know latest songs and be adaptable depending on the evening

READING

Suggested translation:

At the weekend I work in a very small shoe shop. I serve the customers and work on the till. The hours are long and I am tired when I get home. In the future I would like to have my own clothes shop because I am interested in fashion.

6B SKILLS AND PERSONAL QUALITIES (1)

READING

Answers:

1. She doesn't want to earn a lot of money
2. Sporty and likes being outside
3. Dogs
4. Have her own shop/salon for dogs and be a dog trainer
5. She is silly
6. She thinks it is a good idea

READING

Answers:

1. 11 November at 11.11am
2. It was an affectionate name
3. Annoying
4. Writing numbers
5. He had his mobile confiscated in school

EXTRA

Extra:

1. during
2. after
3. quickly
4. it seemed that
5. especially
6. average

LISTENING

Transcript:

Interviewer : Bonjour Monsieur Bernard, vous êtes directeur de l'hôtel Mercure à Lyon. À votre avis, quelles sont les qualités nécessaires d'un directeur d'hôtel ?

M. Bernard : La première image d'un hôtel, c'est le personnel. Il faut que tout le personnel soit disponible et aimable. Le directeur doit être un bon organisateur. Il organise le travail du personnel et doit observer le personnel avec les clients.

Interviewer : Est-ce que les clients sont difficiles ? Est-ce qu'ils se plaignent du service ?

M. Bernard : Dans un hôtel ou un restaurant, il n'y a jamais de problèmes, juste des solutions.

Interviewer : Est-ce qu'il est important de parler des langues étrangères dans votre travail ?

M. Bernard : Oui bien sûr. Nous avons des clients qui viennent de partout dans le monde. L'anglais est essentiel et une connaissance d'une autre langue est désirée.

The correct statements are 1, 4, 6, 7, 10

WRITING

Suggested translation:

Je suis très passionné par mon travail comme directeur de marketing. Le salaire est bon et les heures sont longues. Je passe rarement le week-end en famille. J'aime mon emploi parce qu'il n'y a pas de routine et un jour ne ressemble pas à un autre.

6B SKILLS AND PERSONAL QUALITIES (2)

READING

Answers:

1. b
2. f
3. d
4. c
5. e
6. a

READING

Suggested translation:

I work in a travel agency. I have to book plane tickets for customers and I help them choose a holiday. You need to be relaxed with people and very well organised. It is important to have good geographical knowledge, and being good at maths is essential.

LISTENING

Transcript:

Parler plusieurs langues est vraiment important de nos jours. C'est important pour sa vie personnelle, pour les voyages, les petits jobs à l'étranger et aussi pour la vie professionnelle. La semaine dernière, j'ai dû téléphoner à un client en Espagne pour prendre rendez-vous. Pour maîtriser les langues il faut s'exercer beaucoup. On peut bien sûr apprendre les langues à l'école mais on peut aussi regarder les films en version originale, écouter des chansons sur YouTube et chatter sur Internet. Les langues sont très importantes pour le commerce parce qu'il faut vendre les produits dans la langue des clients.

Answers:

1. Languages
2. Important for personal life e.g. holidays, holiday/part-time jobs abroad, also important for professional life
3. Phone customer in Spain to make an appointment
4. Watching films in original language version, listening to songs on YouTube, chatting on the Internet
5. Languages are important because businesses must sell their products in the customers' own language

READING

Answers:

1. C
2. B
3. A
4. A
5. B
6. B
7. C
8. A
9. D
10. D

6B SKILLS AND PERSONAL QUALITIES (3)

READING

Answers:

1. c
2. i
3. h
4. j
5. a
6. d
7. g
8. e
9. b
10. f

READING

Answers:

1. jours
2. jeunes
3. base
4. emplois
5. écrire
6. est
7. cherchent
8. communiquer
9. clé
10. travailler

EXTRA

Extra:

Include your experiences as well as your qualifications, e.g. photos of you in the rugby team, a letter from an employer confirming your qualities.

LISTENING

Transcript:

Au lycée professionnel de Poitiers, nous avons un stage d'un an pour les étudiants de commerce. Vous ferez six mois en France et quatre mois à l'étranger. Vous aurez le choix entre la Grande-Bretagne, l'Espagne et l'Allemagne.

Il faut se mettre au courant des actualités en France et en Europe en regardant régulièrement la télé, Internet ou en écoutant la radio.

Vous allez travailler en équipe dans un groupe de recherche (quatre personnes maximum) pour faire une présentation à l'oral. Il faut faire attention que deux équipes ne fassent pas le même thème.

Il y aura trois travaux à l'écrit à rendre chaque trimestre, deux en français et un en anglais, espagnol ou allemand (selon le pays de la deuxième partie du stage).

Il y aura plusieurs travaux en équipe où il faut penser rapidement et même temps travailler sans stresse.

Pour s'inscrire, voir nos contacts sur le site web: www.lycéeprofessionnelPoitiers.fr.

Answers:

1. One year
2. Four
3. Great Britain, Spain, Germany
4. News/current affairs
5. Four maximum
6. Oral presentation
7. Not having same topic as another group
8. Three written tasks to hand in each term, two in French and one in the foreign language of place of study
9. Think quickly and not get stressed

6A EMPLOYMENT

6B SKILLS AND PERSONAL QUALITIES

GRAMMAR IN CONTEXT

GRAMMAR

1. PERFECT INFINITIVE

Accept any suitable answers.

2. *DEPUIS*

Suggested translations:

1. I've worked as a waiter for five months.
2. My brother has been studying at university for two years.
3. I've wanted to be a teacher for my whole life.
4. We've been looking for a job for a year and a half.
5. I've been earning money for three years.

3. EMPHATIC PRONOUNS

1. Devant moi
2. Sans eux
3. Chez elle
4. Lui, il l'a fait
5. Je travaille avec elle

4. INDIRECT OBJECT PRONOUNS

1. Elle le leur a donné.
2. Il m'en a parlé.
3. Elle leur donne des bonbons.
4. Elle lui donne des devoirs.

5. DEMONSTRATIVE PRONOUNS

1. Celui-ci
2. Celle-là
3. Celles-là
4. Celui-là
5. Ceux-ci
6. Ceux-là

6. POSSESSIVE PRONOUNS

1. Où est ton sac ? Voici **le mien**.
2. Ma voiture est au garage. Pouvons-nous y aller dans **la vôtre** ?
3. Je ne trouve pas mes clés ? Voici **la tienne**.
4. Voici mes lunettes. Où sont **les siennes ?**
5. Mon patron est très strict. Comment est **le tien ?**
6. Est-ce que tu aimes tes collègues ? **Les miens** sont agréables.

THEME: IDENTITY AND CULTURE

UNIT 3

CUSTOMS AND TRADITIONS

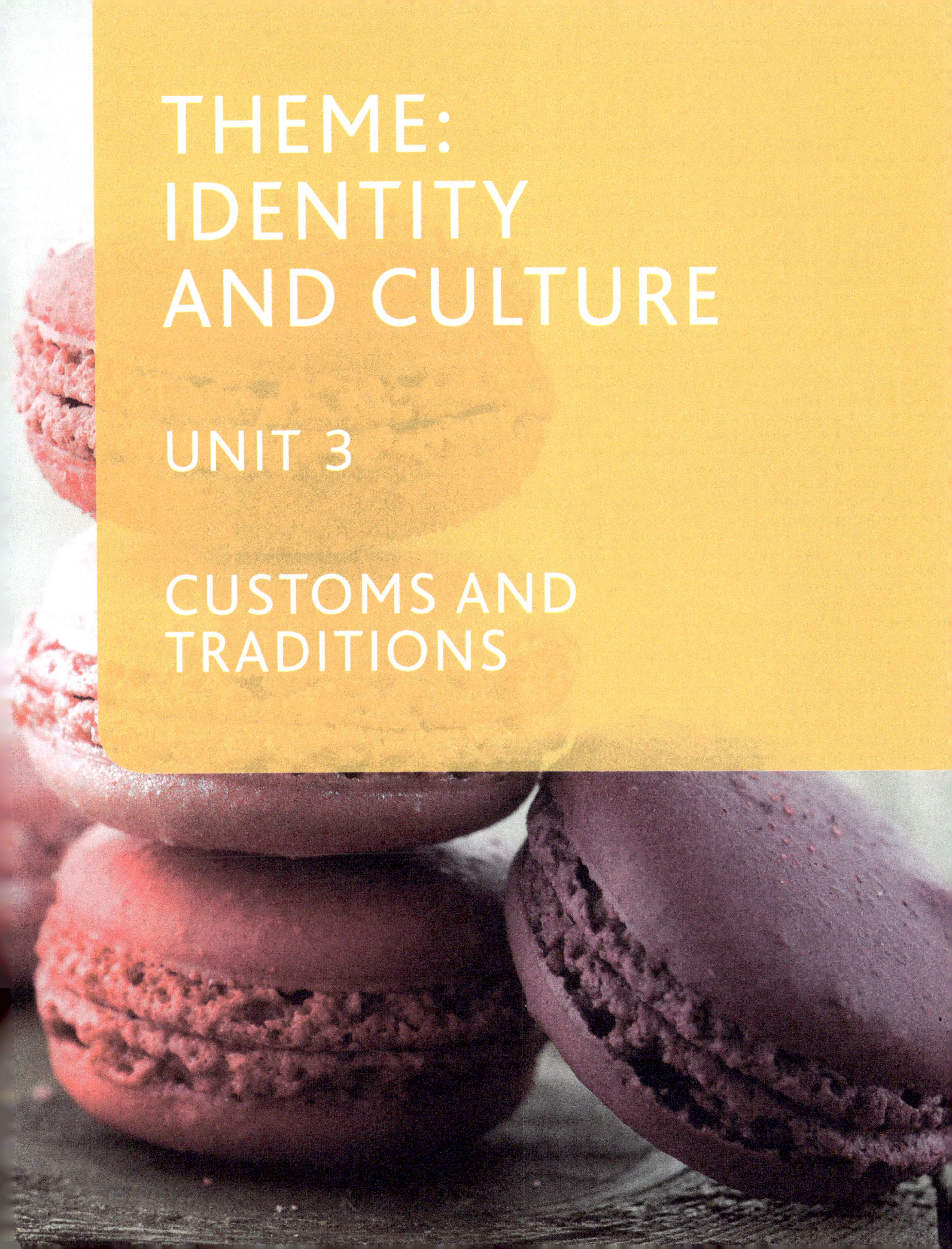

7A FOOD AND DRINK (1)

READING

Answers:

1. e
2. f
3. g
4. h
5. b
6. c
7. i
8. a
9. j
10. d

EXTRA

Extra:

1. I am vegetarian, so I don't eat meat.
2. I am allergic to milk products and cheese.
3. I don't like fish.
4. I am on a diet, so I don't eat chocolate.
5. He doesn't eat sweets because it is bad for one's health.

READING

Answers:

1. Eastern France, Savoy area
2. Winter
3. Friends
4. Potatoes
5. Cheese
6. Ham/sausage/salami
7. Salad

LISTENING

Transcript:

Interviewer : Qu'est-ce que le canelé ?

Boulanger : Le canelé est une pâtisserie traditionnelle de Bordeaux. La recette du canelé est gardée secrète.

Interviewer : Quels sont les ingrédients ?

Boulanger : Les ingrédients de bases sont la farine, les œufs, le lait, le sucre, la vanille et le rhum.

Interviewer : Pourquoi le canelé vient-il de Bordeaux ?

Boulanger : Dans l'histoire les chefs des châteaux ont utilisé les blancs d'œuf et ont voulu jeter les jaunes d'oeuf. Cependant ils ont donné les jaunes d'œuf aux sœurs d'un couvent religieux. Ce sont les sœurs de Bordeaux qui ont inventé le canelé.

Interviewer : Où est-ce qu'on peut acheter le canelé ?

Boulanger : Maintenant le canelé est cuisiné dans les boulangeries de haute qualité à Bordeaux, mais on peut l'acheter en ligne aussi.

Interviewer : La recette date de quand ?

Boulanger : La recette qu'on utilise aujourd'hui est une recette d'il y a vingt-cinq ans.

Answers:

1. a
2. b
3. b
4. a
5. a
6. c

7A FOOD AND DRINK (2)

READING

Answers:

1. A
2. B
3. B
4. D
5. C
6. B
7. A
8. A

READING

Suggested answer:

Usually in France, lunch is taken between midday and 2pm. If you are at home, in school or in a restaurant you have a traditional lunch. Most French people eat a starter, a main course and either some cheese or a dessert. To drink it's always water or wine for adults.

LISTENING

Transcript:

Monsieur, je ne suis pas contente du tout ! Nous avons dû attendre une demi-heure avant d'être servis. Puis le garçon a oublié les boissons. Tous les repas étaient froids et on ne pouvait pas manger la viande parce qu'elle n'était pas bien cuite. On a voulu un dessert mais il ne restait que des glaces !

Et les toilettes sont horribles. Elles sont sales et la lumière ne marche pas. En plus l'addition n'était pas correcte avec quinze euros de plus ! On vous demande une réduction et on ne reviendra jamais. On a déjà laissé un message sur TripAdvisor pour avertir les autres clients !

Answers:

1. Half an hour
2. Drinks
3. Cold
4. Ice cream
5. Toilets
6. Dirty and light didn't work
7. 15 euros
8. Put review on TripAdvisor to warn other customers

Answers:

	Review 1	Review 2	Review 3	Review 4
Date of review	2 August	16 September	10 October	Summer
Opinion	Great view of sea, you must go there if you are on holiday	Excellent service, good relationship with customers	A joy	Prawns not to be missed. Ice creams fantastic
Information	€16.50 for a set menu includes starter, main course and dessert. Seating area outside	Food good quality and good prices	Husband spilt drink on son's pizza and they were given another one for free	View of the sea

7A FOOD AND DRINK (3)

READING

Answers:

1. North African
2. Eastern Algeria
3. Top three favourite meal
4. First World War
5. When soldiers came from Algeria to fight for France
6. Vegetables and meat

LISTENING

Transcript:

Près de vingt pourcent des jeunes français âgés entre quinze à vingt-cinq ans sont obèses. Plus de la moitié des jeunes mangent leur repas devant la télévision, l'ordinateur ou leur tablette pendant qu'ils mangent.

Quelques jeunes Français pensent qu'il est important de manger en famille et d'autres pensent que c'est l'horreur !

Les scientifiques ont prouvé que si les jeunes mangent en famille, ils mangent moins vite et moins que quand ils sont seuls. Un repas de famille autour une table est un des moments où on parle avec tous les membres de la famille en même temps. C'est bon pour la communication et bon pour la santé.

Answers:

1. 20%
2. Watch television, sit in front of computer or tablet
3. Some think it is important and others think it is dreadful
4. They eat less quickly and eat less when they eat with their family
5. So you can talk to your family
6. Communication and health

WRITING

Suggested translations:

1. Je préfère manger en famille autour de la table.
2. J'adore manger dans les restaurants chinois.
3. Hier, j'ai préparé le déjeuner pour mes amis.
4. J'aimerais apprendre à cuisiner dans une école de cuisine.
5. Ma mère est un chef affreux !

READING

Answers:

1. C	4. A	7. A
2. C	5. C	
3. A	6. B	

7B FESTIVALS AND CELEBRATIONS (1)

READING

Answers:

1. What was hiding in his mum's tummy
2. His little brother
3. 16 December
4. 9.33am
5. 49cm
6. He is no longer the youngest

READING

Answers:

1. Odette
2. Emma
3. Irène
4. Julie
5. Benoît
6. Joseph
7. Julie

EXTRA

Extra:

- j'ai passé une nuit blanche
- ma propre voiture
- je ne pouvais pas
- que j'ai jamais vu
- j'ai pris la route

LISTENING

Transcript:

Homme : Félicitations Valérie. J'ai entendu dire que tu vas bientôt te marier. Comment s'appelle ton fiancé ?

Femme : Il s'appelle Bangaly. Il est originaire d'Afrique du Nord.

Homme : Es-tu nerveuse ?

Femme : Ah non. Je suis très contente. Le mariage aura lieu le quinze juillet.

Homme : À quelle heure ?

Femme : Le mariage sera à la Mairie à dix-sept heures.

Homme : Où sera la fête du mariage ?

Femme : Ça sera chez moi, à la ferme.

Answers:

1. Valérie is getting married
2. North Africa
3. Happy
4. 15 July
5. 17.00
6. At Valérie's house on the farm

7B FESTIVALS AND CELEBRATIONS (2)

READING

Answers:

1. d	6. g
2. i	7. h
3. c	8. f
4. b	9. a
5. j	10. e

READING

Answers:

1. 30 July
2. Opening/first concert
3. British
4. 15 July
5. 10 July
6. Musician Moonday died

LISTENING

Transcript:

Le Festival Détours de Babel aura lieu à Grenoble entre le trente et un mars et le seize avril. Pendant dex-sept jours, le festival de musique présentera plusieurs genres de musique, dont le rock, la pop, le jazz, le classique et la soul. Vous pouvez venir écouter la musique mondiale.

Un concert de rock ouvrira le festival et un concert classique le terminera.

L'entrée au festival est gratuite. Les billets de concert coûtent entre cinq et vingt-huit euros.

Answers:

Ville	Grenoble
Dates du festival	31 mars–16 avril
Genres de musique	Rock, pop, jazz, classique, soul
Concert d'ouverture	Rock
Concert final	Classique
Prix	Entrée gratuite. Billets 5–28 €

READING

Suggested translation:

The music festival in Lille took place between 20–30 May. I went there with my friends and we slept in a tent. It was the first time I had gone away without my parents. It was an unforgettable weekend!

7B FESTIVALS AND CELEBRATIONS (3)

READING

Answers:

1. ouvre
2. printemps
3. plus
4. sud
5. sera
6. ouverture
7. chaîne
8. semaine
9. vedettes

READING

Answers:

1. Doesn't watch films any more, she listens to them
2. Pictures, settings, faces
3. Faces
4. She knew the actors
5. Muscly with blond hair

LISTENING

Transcript:

Cet été entre le premier août et le dix août, venez à Lorient à l'ouest de la Bretagne pour le Festival Interceltique. Cette année, c'est l'année du Pays de Galles. Vous pouvez regarder les danseurs folkloriques, écouter de la musique et goûter les produits gallois.

Le festival Interceltique se passe tous les ans ici et l'entrée est gratuite. Il faut seulement payer pour quelques concerts. Hier, dans le Grand Théâtre, la chanteuse Suzanne Vega a fait son premier concert de l'an. Elle a présenté son huitième album devant beaucoup de spectateurs. Ce soir au Palais des Congrès, c'est le tour de la harpiste Cécile Corbel qui chante aussi avec sa douce voix.

Answers:

1. 1–10 August
2. Lorient, west Brittany
3. Wales
4. See dancing, listen to music, eat products from Wales
5. Free to enter, pay for concerts
6. Eighth
7. Harp
8. Sing

WRITING

Answers:

1. Le festival a une bonne ambiance.
2. Beaucoup de touristes sont venus au festival de musique l'année dernière.
3. Je vais au cinéma avec mes amis pour faire la fête.
4. Je voudrais aller à un festival de film.
5. L'année prochaine je ferai du camping au festival.

7A FOOD AND DRINK

7B FESTIVALS AND CELEBRATIONS

GRAMMAR IN CONTEXT

GRAMMAR

1. ADVERBS: QUANTIFIERS AND INTENSIFIERS

Suggested translations:

1. Mon frère a bu trop de coca.
2. Il fait très chaud pendant le festival.
3. Ils aiment boire un peu de vin avec leur repas.
4. Il y avait beaucoup de touristes.
5. J'ai mangé assez de chocolat.

2. ADVERBS OF PLACE AND TIME

1. Le concert se trouve **loin** du centre.
2. Tous les concerts ont lieu **dehors**.
3. **Hier** je suis allé à une boum.
4. J'ai **déjà** assisté à beaucoup de concerts.
5. Pendant le festival il y a des touristes **partout**.
6. **Après-demain** nous irons au marché.

3. EXPRESSION OF QUANTITIES USING *DE*

1. Une boîte de café
2. Une bouteille d'eau
3. Un paquet de biscuits
4. Une tablette de chocolat
5. Un pot de yaourt

4. ADVERBS: COMPARATIVES AND SUPERLATIVES

Suggested translations:

1. Le gâteau était le plus délicieux.
2. Le festival était le pire.
3. Je suis le/la plus rapide.
4. Mon frère est le plus gentil.
5. Le chocolat est le mieux.
6. Je dépense plus d'argent que ma sœur.

5. PERFECT TENSE WITH REFLEXIVE VERBS

Accept any suitable paragraph in the perfect tense which includes the reflexive verbs listed.

6. *EN, AU, AUX, À LA*

1. Le festival a lieu **en** France.
2. J'adore les restaurants **à** Paris.
3. Les touristes vont **en** ville.
4. Il y a beaucoup de restaurants typiques **au** Portugal.
5. Il travaille **aux** États-Unis.

THEME: WALES AND THE WORLD – AREAS OF INTEREST

UNIT 3

GLOBAL SUSTAINABILITY

8A ENVIRONMENT (1)

READING

Answers:

1. g	6. b
2. j	7. d
3. i	8. h
4. f	9. a
5. c	10. e

READING

Answers:

1. People who have respect for the environment
2. Waste/rubbish
3. Mountains, forests, plains, rivers, sea
4. Cleaning house
5. How many plates/meals are thrown away?
6. Men, women, children, young ladies

READING

Suggested translations:

1. Recycling nuclear waste is very dangerous and expensive.
2. Amazon forests are destroyed for their wood.
3. Plants, birds and fish die in polluted water.
4. The greenhouse effect warms up the earth.
5. There are more floods and droughts in the world today.

LISTENING

Transcript:

L'effet de serre est causé par les émissions de gaz carbonique. La terre se réchauffe et il y a des inondations et des sécheresses.

Une marée noire est très dangereuses et elle peut tuer des millions de poissons et d'oiseaux.

La pluie acide est causée par les émissions des usines et des automobiles. Les gaz se transforment en acides et quand ils sont mélangés avec la pluie, cela tue la végétation.

Answers:

1. est	6. tuer
2. carbonique	7. oiseaux
3. terre	8. pluie
4. inondations	9. usines
5. noire	10. quand

8A ENVIRONMENT (2)

READING

Answers:

Colour bags	Yellow	Black	Blue
Items that go in the bag	Empty plastic bottles, small cardboard packaging, tins, cans, foil containers, empty aerosols	Plastic bags, yoghurt pots, cardboard plates, light bulbs, plastic cups, plastic tubs	Paper, newspapers, magazines
Collection dates	Tuesday, Saturday July and August	Friday July and August	Thursday July and August

LISTENING

Transcript:

La plupart de nos déchets ne sont pas biodégradables et ils prennent de nombreuses années à se décomposer. Voici des statistiques :

Les vêtements en nylon prennent trente à quarante ans à se décomposer.

Pour le papier et le journal, cela prend deux à trois mois et pour un chewing-gum c'est cinq ans !

Un des pires, ce sont les sacs ou les bouteilles en plastique qui prennent cent à cinq cents ans à se décomposer !

Les pires, ce sont les bouteilles en verre qui prennent quatre mille ans à disparaître et les piles qui prennent huit mille ans !

Answers:

Items	How long it takes to decompose
Clothes (nylon)	30–40 years
Paper	2–3 months
Chewing gum	5 years
Plastic bags and bottles	100–500 years
Glass bottles	4,000 years
Batteries	8,000 years

READING

Answers:

1. vacances
2. être
3. petits
4. recyclage
5. année
6. recycler
7. coûte
8. facile
9. mains
10. heures
11. pleut
12. école

8A ENVIRONMENT (3)

READING

Answers:

1. soleil
2. vent
3. eau
4. biomasse
5. chaleur

LISTENING

Transcript

Selon l'organisation de Greenpeace, la France montre des impacts de changements climatiques. L'impact le plus inquiétant est la hausse de températures en France. Il y a des preuves qui indiquent que certaines régions de la France peuvent connaître une hausse de trois pourcent d'ici la fin du siècle.

On voit déjà en France l'augmentation de la température de la surface de la mer dans le sud et la réduction de la couverture neigeuse dans les Alpes et les Pyrénées. Dans les Alpes, le glacier Rhône est en retraite. De plus en plus, l'hiver est plus court et l'été est plus long.

Answers:

1. France is seeing the impact of climate change
2. Increase in temperature
3. 3%
4. Increase in sea temperature and reduction in snow lying areas such as the Alps and the Pyrenees
5. It is retreating/shrinking
6. Winters are shorter summers are longer

READING

Answers:

The correct statements are 2, 4, 6, 8, 9

WRITING

Suggested translations:

1. On doit penser à l'avenir.
2. Tu devrais recycler.
3. Il faut utiliser le train au lieu de la voiture.
4. À mon avis, c'est la responsabilité de tout le monde.
5. Il faut protéger l'environnement.

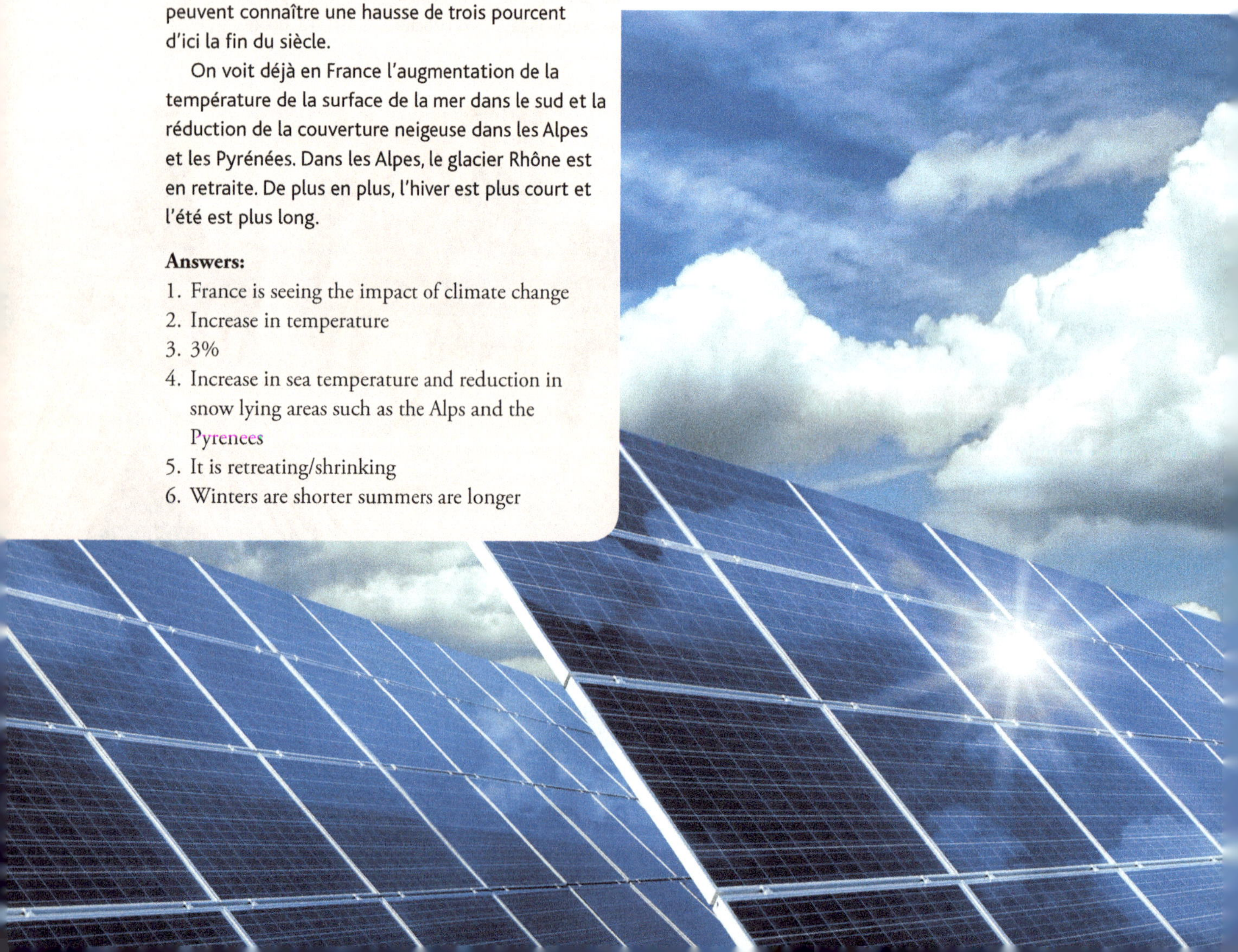

8B SOCIAL ISSUES (1)

READING

Answers:

1. Pauvres : 5,000,000–8,000,000
2. Sans domicile fixe : 130,000
3. Femmes : 17%
4. -25 ans : 20%
5. 16–18 ans de femmes : 70%

LISTENING

Teachers will need to give the phrase – 'viande de brousse' (bush meat).

Transcript:

L'épidémie d'Ebola qui a sa source en Afrique de l'Ouest a presque disparu en Côte d'Ivoire. Pour aider à contrôler le virus, le gouvernement a interdit à la population de vendre ou de manger la viande de brousse.

En plus, les marchés forains ont été interdits pour éviter les grandes foules. Un problème difficile à contrôler parce qu'il y a beaucoup de villages qui ne sont pas très faciles à joindre et qui sont aussi sans eau, sans électricité et donc sans informations.

Answers:

1. West Africa
2. Eat or sell
3. Markets
4. Prevent large crowds
5. Water, electricity

READING

Suggested translation:

Can you help the homeless in Lyon? We would like to invite you to bring blankets and sleeping bags that are in good condition to the town hall. A small gesture is very important to help the poor people in our town.

READING

Answers:

1. Streets, train stations, Metro, car parks, under bridges
2. 2006
3. Tents
4. 200
5. Hunger, health, unemployment, alcoholism, drugs, death

8B SOCIAL ISSUES (2)

READING

Answers:

1. 73%
2. 41%
3. 37%
4. 10%
5. 11%
6. Town centre, suburbs, Metro

READING

Answers:

1. Hunger and violence
2. Two years ago
3. Showed him/her around the apartment
4. Four
5. 15
6. Prison
7. Work or rest

WRITING

Suggested translation:

Cette année au lycée, nous avons gagné presque mille livres sterling pour les réfugiés en Afrique. Pour gagner de l'argent nous avons eu un concert. Les élèves plus âgés ont joué un match de football contre les profs. Les profs ont perdu !

LISTENING

Transcript:

L'Opération Enfant Noël vous permet d'être le père noël pour un enfant défavorisé dans un pays pauvre, un pays où il y a la guerre, ou un pays touché par une catastrophe.

L'année dernière, une organisation en Suisse a collecté plus de onze mille cadeaux de noël pour la Moldavie.

Les cadeaux sont donnés dans des boîtes à chaussures. Vous pouvez en donner jusqu'au quinze novembre. Cette année, il y aura cent cinquante endroits de collecte partout en Suisse.

Dans les cartons on peut mettre des jouets, des bonbons et des brosses à dents. On ne peut pas mettre du chocolat ni des livres avec des mots. Les livres avec juste des images sont acceptés.

Il y a trois catégories de boîte par tranche d'âge, les deux à quatre ans, les cinq à neuf ans et les dix à quatorze ans. Il faut aussi distinguer entre garçons et filles.

The correct statements are 3, 4, 6, 8, 10

EXTRA

Extra:

9. You can put reading books in the boxes.
10. You can give presents to teenagers.

8B SOCIAL ISSUES (3)

READING

Answers:

1. Are you a pupil at a *lycée*? Are you aged between 16 and 18? Do you want to make changes?
2. 1,000
3. Disadvantaged children
4. Via the website

READING

Answers:

1. b
2. b
3. a
4. a
5. c
6. c

LISTENING

Transcript:

Jacques : Qu'est-ce qu'on va faire cette année pour gagner de l'argent pour notre association pour les personnes âgées ?

Sylvie : Oui, les personnes âgées sont souvent seules et cela serait bien si on pouvait les aider. Alors moi j'aimerais organiser un déjeuner pour les personnes âgées de notre ville. Peut-être que notre classe peut apporter de quoi manger et à boire.

Jacques : Bonne idée ! Je vais organiser le transport avec les profs et les parents. Le groupe de jazz peut jouer pendant le déjeuner ?

Sylvie : Ça serait chouette! Qu'est-ce que tu vas apporter comme plats ?

Jacques : Mon père est boulanger, donc je peux apporter du pain.

Sylvie : Moi, j'adore faire des desserts. Je pense que je ferai une tarte aux fraises. Alors, il faut qu'on demande la permission au directeur avant de l'organiser.

Answers:

1. Old aged people
2. They are often alone
3. Lunch
4. Transport
5. Bread
6. Strawberry tart
7. Head teacher

8A ENVIRONMENT
8B SOCIAL ISSUES
GRAMMAR IN CONTEXT

GRAMMAR

1. INDEFINITE PRONOUNS

Suggested translations:

1. Someone has left the tap on.
2. I have eaten something new.
3. Somewhere in the world.
4. Everyone must recycle.
5. No one wants to recycle.

2. THE PASSIVE

Suggested translations:

1. The water was polluted.
2. The birds were killed.
3. The paper is recycled.
4. The dinner has been eaten.
5. The recycling is done.

3. *DEPUIS*

Suggested translations:

1. J'apprends le français depuis cinq ans.
2. Il est ici depuis une semaine.
3. Il habitait en Espagne depuis six mois.
4. Ils recyclaient depuis dix ans.
5. L'usine polluait la rivière depuis vingt ans.

4. USEFUL VERBS

Accept any suitable sentence using the following verbs:

- *subventionner* – to subsidise
- *aider* – to help
- *protéger* – to protect
- *provoquer* – to cause
- *réduire* – to reduce
- *endommager* – to damage
- *ralentir* – to slow down
- *soutenir* – to support

5. REVISING TENSES

Suggested translations:

1. Present: We do lots of things to improve the environment.
2. Perfect: My friends gave their pocket money to the organisation.
3. Pluperfect: Alex had bought fair trade products.
4. Conditional: My father would like an electric car.
5. Imperfect: In the past we were less responsible.
6. Future: I will do more things to help others.

6. USING A VARIETY OF ADJECTIVES

Accept any suitable sentences using the following adjectives:

- *mondial* – global
- *dangereux* – dangerous
- *nocif* – harmful
- *grave* – serious
- *sec* – dry
- *inquiétant* – worrying

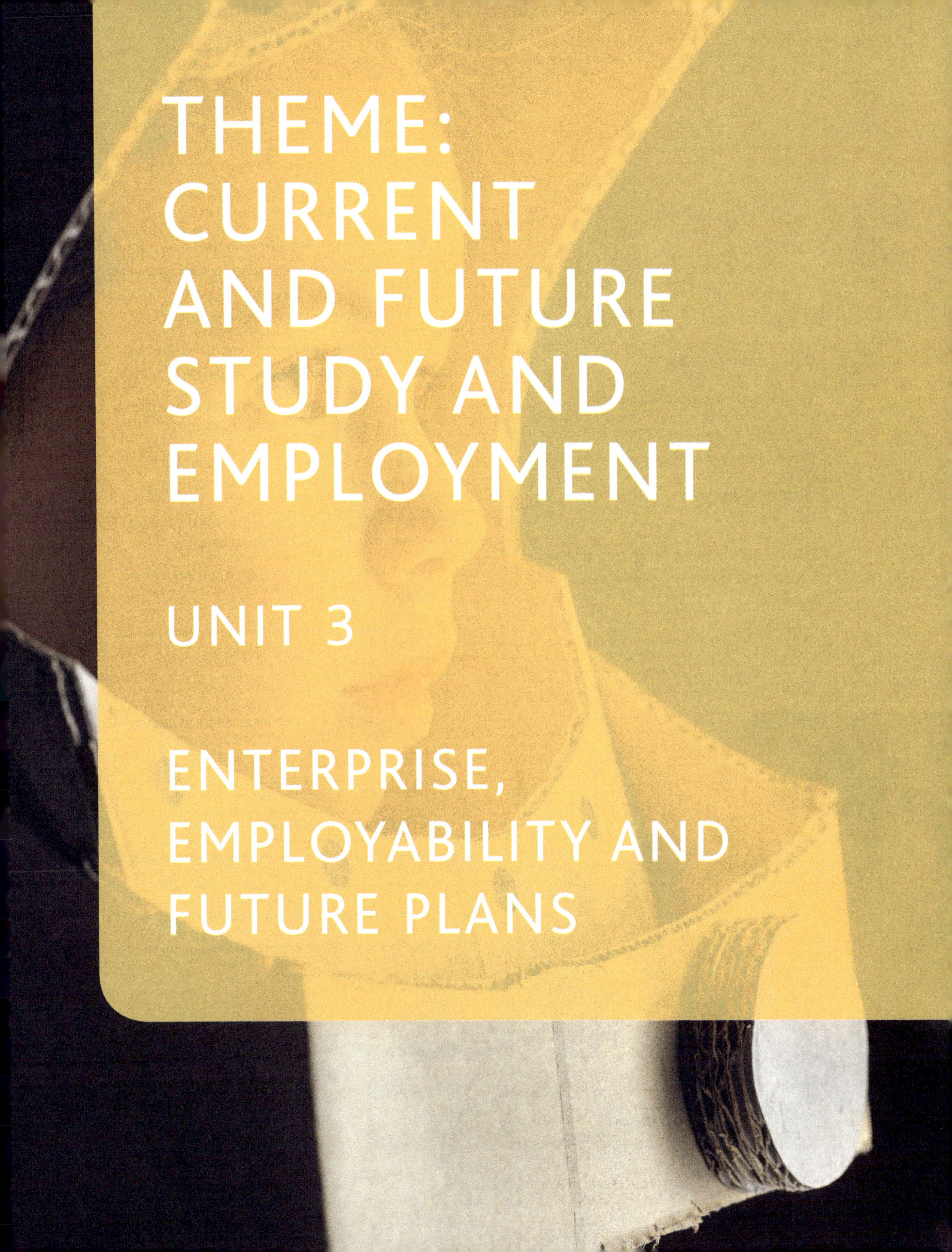

THEME: CURRENT AND FUTURE STUDY AND EMPLOYMENT

UNIT 3

ENTERPRISE, EMPLOYABILITY AND FUTURE PLANS

9A POST-16 STUDY (1)

READING

Answers:

a. 4	d. 2	g. 6
b. 3	e. 1	h. 1
c. 1	f. 5	i. 4

READING

Answers:

Day of forum: Tuesday	
Type of work available: Voluntary	
Number of employers present last year	20
Number of employers this year	16
Documents the young people need to take to the forum	CV and application letter

LISTENING

Transcript:

Jamie : Moi, je suis plutôt scientifique. Je me suis toujours orienté vers le monde scientifique et je voudrais combiner au mieux ma passion pour les sciences et mon désir d'aider à la société.

Laure : J'aimerais voyager. J'apprécie beaucoup les autres cultures et j'ai envie de voir le monde.

Lily : Après avoir réussi mon bac, j'espère aller à l'université afin d'étudier les maths.

Georges : Je voudrais parler couramment l'espagnol et le français.

André : Moi, je chercherai un travail bien payé car à mon avis le salaire est important.

Sophie : Les sports sont importants pour moi parce que j'aime bouger !

Guillaume : Quant à une carrière... Je ne sais pas encore. Je n'ai pas fait mon choix.

Suggested answers:

Jamie : Médecin – aime les sciences et veut aider

Laure : Hôtesse de l'air – aime voyager

Lily : Dirigeant d'une banque – aime les maths

Georges : Traducteur – aime les langues

André : Dirigeant d'une entreprise – voudrait beaucoup d'argent

Sophie : Monitrice de natation – est sportive

Guillaume : (Any job as has not made up mind)

9A POST-16 STUDY (2)

READING

Answers:

1. i	4. a	7. g
2. e	5. f	8. b
3. c	6. h	9. d

EXTRA

Extra:

1. Find out information at the careers evening.
2. Have a discussion with our students.
3. Every Friday in March.

READING

Answers:

1. Write letters
2. Bring cups of coffee
3. Not long/just started
4. Serious
5. 8.30am
6. Coffee with milk
7. Green tea/black coffee
8. Polite and charming

LISTENING

Transcript:

En premier vous pouvez faire des études dans l'Hôtellerie. Ces études sont bonnes si vous voulez travailler à l'accueil d'un hôtel, dans la restauration ou l'hébergement.

Après avoir fait des études spécialisées en seconde vous pouvez vous inscrire aux études dans l'Hôtellerie. Il y aura une sélection à l'entrée. C'est un bon choix pour étudier à côté des autres matières, telles que le français, les maths, l'histoire, l'économie, le droit et la gestion. Les langues sont essentielles si vous voulez travailler dans cette industrie.

Pendant les études il faut faire au moins huit semaines en entreprise.

Answers:

1. Year 12/sixth form
2. Hotel reception, restaurant or in accommodation
3. Year 11
4. Any from: French, maths, history, economics, law, management
5. Languages
6. Work for a company

WRITING

Suggested translation:

Cette année j'ai travaillé dur au lycée. J'aimerais revenir en première en septembre. J'espère étudier l'espagnol, le français et l'anglais. Dans deux ans, j'aimerais aller à l'université et je voudrais aussi étudier à l'étranger.

READING

Suggested translations:

1. I don't know exactly what I will study.
2. In my opinion, sciences are important.
3. Chemistry and maths are subjects that go well together.
4. I will have to work very hard.
5. If I have good marks I will carry on with my business studies.

9A POST-16 STUDY (3)

READING

Answers:

1. b
2. e
3. h
4. d
5. f
6. c
7. g
8. a

READING

Answers:

1. répondre
2. devez
3. faut
4. répondez
5. précise
6. une
7. capable
8. équipe
9. expérience
10. positif
11. vos
12. partagez
13. mamie
14. positive
15. vous
16. forts
17. adjectives
18. longtemps

LISTENING

Transcript:

Directeur : Bonjour Madame et bienvenue au club de sport.

Magali : Enchantée.

Directeur : Veuillez vous asseoir ici. Alors, Je voudrais commencer par votre CV. Vous avez dit avoir de l'expérience avec les enfants ?

Magali : Oui, pendant mes études de sport au lycée, j'ai passé un an comme monitrice de football tous les mercredis et vendredis après-midi. En plus j'ai passé les six semaines de l'été en Espagne pour améliorer mes compétences en langues.

Directeur : C'est bien. Alors, qu'avez-vous fait exactement quand vous étiez monitrice ?

Magali : J'ai travaillé avec les enfants de trois à huit ans. J'ai dû les aider à faire des exercices d'échauffement avant de jouer au football. J'ai fait l'appel et j'ai aussi préparé le terrain de football. J'ai dû me lever tôt le matin pour être à l'heure. À mon avis il est important d'être ponctuel et organisé.

Directeur : Avez-vous des questions à nous poser ?

Magali : Oui, quelles sont les heures du travail ?

Directeur : Les heures sont le samedi de sept heures à quatorze heures.

Answers:

1. Children
2. Football instructor
3. Wednesday and Friday afternoon
4. Summer
5. Improve her language skills
6. Three to eight years
7. Took register and prepared the pitch
8. Punctual and organised
9. What are the working hours?

9B CAREER PLANS (1)

READING

Suggested answers:

Université	Travail	Les deux
1, 4, 5, 7	2, 6, 8	3, 9, 10

EXTRA

Extra – suggested translations:

2. Having a job allows you to earn money.
3. It prepares you to be more independent.
5. You tend to work alone.
6. You tend to work in a team.

READING

Answers:

1. Study German
2. Year 10–11
3. Six months
4. March–August
5. Based on exchange between two families
6. Enriching experience, improve language skills, no cost
7. Don't see family for six months

LISTENING

Transcript:

Voulez-vous être technicien d'informatique ? Notre diplôme se passe à Nantes pendant deux ans. Les études commencent en septembre. Si le programme vous intéresse il y a une sélection d'entrée le quatre juin. Un dossier d'inscription est disponible sur notre site web, www.asktechnantes.eu. Si vous venez nous voir il y aura une soirée le vingt-deux mai à partir de dix-neuf heures où vous pourrez rencontrer des étudiants de cette année.

Answers:

1. ICT technician
2. Two years
3. September
4. Selection for a place on the course
5. Application pack
6. 22 May
7. 19.00
8. Students from this year

9B CAREER PLANS (2)

READING

Answers:

1. 19%
2. 43%
3. 15%
4. 26%
5. 70%
6. 17%
7. Quality of life

READING

Answers:

The correct statements are 2, 3, 4, 8, 10

WRITING

Suggested translation:

Aimerais-tu travailler à l'étranger ? Oui, peut-être que je passerai un an en France en tant qu'assistant dans une école. Je ne veux pas être professeur, mais j'aime travailler avec les enfants. J'ai vraiment besoin d'améliorer mes compétences linguistiques.

LISTENING

Transcript:

Un « au pair » s'occupe des enfants en famille. D'habitude les « au pair » habitent avec la famille et ils aident aussi à faire le ménage. L'avantage principal de ce travail est qu'on apprend la langue très vite. Faites attention aux familles qui veulent un domestique !

Avant de commencer il est important de discuter des tâches que vous ferez pour la famille. Si vous avez déjà fait du babysitting ou fait du travail avec les enfants, ces expériences seront un avantage. Selon la loi en France, un au pair ne peut pas avoir la responsabilité d'un enfant de moins de deux ans.

D'habitude la durée de l'emploi est entre deux mois et trois ans.

Les tâches normales sont :

- Aller chercher les enfants à l'école.
- Jouer avec les enfants.
- Préparer et donner à manger aux petits.
- Ranger les chambres des enfants.
- Faire du babysitting le soir.

Answers:

1. Looking after children and doing some housework
2. Learn the language quickly
3. Not becoming a servant
4. Agree with the family what your duties are
5. Have responsibility for a child under 2 years old
6. Two months
7. Any three from: taking and fetching children from school, playing with children, preparing and feeding the children, tidying children's bedrooms, babysitting in the evening

9B CAREER PLANS (3)

READING

Answers:

1. Germaine
2. Hervé
3. Germaine, Régis, Thierry
4. Régis
5. Annie
6. Paul
7. Paul
8. Hervé

READING

Answers:

1. Holidays
2. Have a gap year
3. Four corners of the world
4. Rucksack
5. To have fun
6. 6pm
7. Took some pens and a note pad from her cupboard

READING

Suggested translation:

Later in life I would like to be a pilot because I am interested in planes. Before that I would like to travel in Australia as I have family there. I have to earn some money before leaving. I intend to find a summer job.

LISTENING

Transcript:

Yvette : Mon rêve serait d'habiter en France. Avant, j'espère voyager dans le monde entier, découvrir des traditions différentes et goûter de la nouvelle nourriture.

Marcel : J'aimerais aller à l'université à la Sorbonne à Paris, mais cela dépendra des résultats que j'obtiendrai au bac.

Tatiana : Je voudrais parler couramment l'espagnol et l'allemand parce que je voudrais travailler à l'étranger.

Nina : Moi, je voudrais faire du travail bénévole. J'aimerais voyager et en même temps aider les autres.

Gaston : Après avoir fait mon bac, j'ai l'intention de prendre une année sabbatique en Angleterre ou aux États-Unis, pour me perfectionner en anglais.

Answers:

1. Marcel
2. Tatiana, Gaston
3. Yvette, Tatiana, Nina, Gaston
4. Nina
5. Yvette
6. Marcel, Gaston

9A POST-16 STUDY
9B CAREER PLANS
GRAMMAR IN CONTEXT

GRAMMAR

1. TALKING ABOUT THE FUTURE IN DIFFERENT WAYS

Accept any suitable response that uses all of the structures correctly.

2. BASIC ACCURACY

1. J'aimerais continuer mes études.
2. Mon frère voudrait travailler à l'étranger.
3. Après mes examens j'irai en vacances.
4. Mes parents disent que l'université est importante.
5. L'année prochaine je chercherai un travail.

3. ILLUSTRATING POINTS AND EXPRESSING OPINIONS

Accept any suitable opinions on the topic.

4. WRITING A LETTER OF APPLICATION

Accept any suitable answer for each sentence.

5. *PENDANT* – FOR/DURING

Suggested translations:

1. J'ai travaillé dans un bureau pendant une semaine.
2. Il a joué dans l'équipe pendant deux ans.
3. J'ai travaillé comme au pair pendant un an.
4. Nous avons étudié le français pendant six ans

6. REVISING YOUR TENSES

Accept suitable answers in the following tenses:

1. Present
2. Simple/immediate future
3. Future
4. Conditional
5. Perfect
6. Imperfect

IMAGE CREDITS

Icons: Reading, Listening, Speaking, Writing, Extra, Grammar, Lightbulb, Vocabulary, © schinsilord – Fotolia.

Pages 46–47, © JB Fontana – Fotolia. Page 48, © micromonkey – Fotolia. Page 49, © Milkos – Fotolia. Page 50, © stadelpeter – Fotolia. Page 52, © Photograohee.eu – Fotolia. Page 53, © lassedesignen – Fotolia. Page 54, © JackF – Fotolia. Page 55, © Jack F – Fotolia. Page 57, © ALDECAstudio – Fotolia. Page 58, © Grigory Bruev – Fotolia. Page 59, © nevskyphoto – Fotolia. Page 61, © lucadp – Fotolia. Page 62, © VRD – Fotolia. Page 63, © sebra – Fotolia. Page 64, © monkeybusiness – Fotolia. Page 66, © fullempty – Fotolia. Page 67, © Christian Schwier – Fotolia. Page 69, © Tom Wang – Fotolia. Page 70, © David Pereiras – Fotolia. Page 71, © Brian Jackson – Fotolia. Page 72, © BillionPhotos.com – Fotolia. Page 73, © freshidea – Fotolia. Page 74, © yatcenko – Fotolia. Page 75, © WaveBreakMediaMicro – Fotolia. Page 76, © Andrey Popov – Fotolia. Page 77, © Focus Pocus LTD – Fotolia. Page 78, © determined – Fotolia. Page 79, © Black Spring – Fotolia. Page 81, © berc – Fotolia. Page 82, © Delphotostock – Fotolia. Page 83, © zhu difeng – Fotolia. Page 84, © russieseo – Fotolia. Page 85 © Dominique VERNIER – Fotolia. Page 86, © paolo maria airenti – Fotolia. Page 87, © mikola249 – Fotolia. Page 88, © zhu difeng – Fotolia. Page 89, © Tamara Kulikova – Fotolia. Page 90, © monkeybusiness – Fotolia. Page 91, © Mila Supynnska – Fotolia. Page 92, © goodluz – Fotolia. Page 93, © djile – Fotolia. Page 94, © soloveyigor – Fotolia. Page 95, © Iuliia Metkalova – Fotolia. Page 96, © david_franklin – Fotolia. Page 98 © Robert Kneschke – Fotolia. Page 99, © LuckyImages – Fotolia. Page 100, © Mik Man – Fotolia. Page 101, © JackF – Fotolia. Page 102, © eddygaleotti – Fotolia. Page 103, © peshkov – Fotolia. Page 104, © korionov – Fotolia. Page 105, © icsnaps – Fotolia. Page 106, © Smileus – Fotolia. Page 107, © Halfpoint – Fotolia. Page 108, © sanchos303 – Fotolia. Page 109, © niroworld – Fotolia. Page 111, © Konstantin Yuganov – Fotolia. Page 112, © Syda Productions – Fotolia. Page 113, © vege – Fotolia. Page 114, © connel_design – Fotolia. Page 115, © javiindy – Fotolia. Page 116, © Olivier Le Moal – Fotolia. Page 117, © faithie – Fotolia. Page 118, © Kanashkin – Fotolia.

TRACK LISTING

Module 1A(1)	Track 1
Module 1A(2)	Track 2
Module 1A(3)	Track 3
Module 1B(1)	Track 4
Module 1B(2)	Track 5
Module 1B(3)	Track 6
Module 2A(1)	Track 7
Module 2A(2)	Track 8
Module 2A(3)	Track 9
Module 2B(1)	Track 10
Module 2B(2)	Track 11
Module 2B(3)	Track 12
Module 3A(1)	Track 13
Module 3A(2)	Track 14
Module 3A(3)	Track 15
Module 3B(1)	Track 16
Module 3B(2)	Track 17
Module 3B(3)	Track 18
Module 4A(1)	Track 19
Module 4A(2)	Track 20
Module 4A(3)	Track 21
Module 4B(1)	Track 22
Module 4B(2)	Track 23
Module 4B(3)	Track 24
Module 5A(1)	Track 25
Module 5A(2)	Track 26
Module 5A(3)	Track 27
Module 5B(1)	Track 28
Module 5B(2)	Track 29
Module 5B(3)	Track 30
Module 6A(1)	Track 31
Module 6A(2)	Track 32
Module 6A(3)	Track 33
Module 6B(1)	Track 34
Module 6B(2)	Track 35
Module 6B(3)	Track 36
Module 7A(1)	Track 37
Module 7A(2)	Track 38
Module 7A(3)	Track 39
Module 7B(1)	Track 40
Module 7B(2)	Track 41
Module 7B(3)	Track 42
Module 8A(1)	Track 43
Module 8A(2)	Track 44
Module 8A(3)	Track 45
Module 8B(1)	Track 46
Module 8B(2)	Track 47
Module 8B(3)	Track 48
Module 9A(1)	Track 49
Module 9A(2)	Track 50
Module 9A(3)	Track 51
Module 9B(1)	Track 52
Module 9B(2)	Track 53
Module 9B(3)	Track 54

Lightning Source UK Ltd.
Milton Keynes UK
UKOW07f2053021117
312045UK00001B/2/P